Simulation Games
and Learning Activities Kit
for the Elementary School

Simulation Games
and Learning Activities Kit
for the Elementary School

Jay Reese

Parker Publishing Company, Inc.
West Nyack, New York

© 1977, *by*

PARKER PUBLISHING COMPANY, INC.

West Nyack, N.Y.

Library of Congress Cataloging in Publication Data

Reese, Jay,
    Simulation games and learning activities kit
for the elementary school.

    Bibliography: p.
    Includes index.
    1. Educational games. 2. Simulated environment
(Teaching method) I. Title.
LB1029.G3R43   372.4'14   76-52500
ISBN 0-13-810515-4

Printed in the United States of America

To Mary Lois, my wife.

To my parents, who encouraged and played games with their four boys.

To my principals: Tom Putnam, Phil Berg, and Mary Louise Noble, for allowing me to create and use simulations and games in my classes.

How This Book Will Provide You with a Uniquely Effective Teaching Program . . .

The use of simulations and games in the classroom is increasing among experienced educators, and for good reason. In high school and college classrooms, simulations have been in use for several years and have proven both popular and effective. They can be just as effective in the elementary grades, provided teachers find good ones that are tailored for students of these ages. This book will help to fill that need.

Habits and attitudes formed in elementary grades grow more definite, more "set," as students grow older. Good study habits, good classroom attitudes, will aid students in the upper grades and college, while the reverse will hinder and eventually lead to dropouts—mentally, if not physically. As most of us know, school dropouts are a perennial problem, and many of these students *can* be turned on to school by the use of simulations and games. Moreover, good students also benefit from the accelerated learning progress these techniques can bring.

One of the key factors in determining a student's attitude toward school is boredom, and this inevitably results when students are not challenged in one way or another. To some students, boredom equals school and school equals boredom. There is no "easy" road to learning many of the basic facts and skills, and such learning can indeed be boring. Yet if a student can look forward to a dramatically exciting class period during the day, if he has this bright spot to hold his interest, the surge of interest can carry over to other classes and a potential dropout may be persuaded to stay in. The "average" student will find that school is a far more pleasant and interesting place, and the bright student will find that school *is* relevant to life.

Of various claims made for the use of simulations and games, the one that has the least amount of argument is that students become *involved.* Any teacher who has tried a good simulation game in his or her classroom will attest to this. Involvement, enthusiasm, and empathy are present. One such game may not be magic for every student, but a group or series of simulations and games will reach all but a very few. You will see students discussing strategies and plans in their free time—and outside the classroom as well. They will actually become so interested they won't want the class period to end.

For example, I found this to be the case when I was testing the simulation LANDOSA (given in full in Chapter 4). As the monetary inflation in the game grew more acute, and the imaginary president of the nation could not control it, students in the sixth-grade room booed the president's name. There was talk of a revolution. When the president was finally removed from office, they cheered. But then they became the Landosan Senate, trying to solve the inflation problem themselves, and they found it was not as easy as they thought. Ideas and proposals came thick and fast. Lunch time came, and they didn't want to end the discussion. They finally decided that research was needed. They carried on the discussion and arguments into the lunchroom, and into the music period after lunch recess as well. The following day, some of the students came back with examples of how present-day nations tried (and are trying) to control inflation. The Landosan Senate adopted one of them, after a vigorous discussion. . . . *No one* could say that this class was not involved. From this simulation they learned what inflation is, how it affected their lives (and buying power), what keeps inflation going, and how hard it is to stop. They also developed greater research skill, debating skills—and learned how to make group decisions.

And you the teacher, too, will become involved. It will be the bright spot in your day when you use simulations. If the teacher is excited, students will be, too. In a good simulation game, the teacher has a new role—one of director, facilitator, and arranger. You are no longer lecturing students, or merely giving assignments. You are guiding them, helping them, by making the simulation go easier. You will still be as busy as ever, maybe busier—but every classroom will become far more interesting . . . and more productive.

The simulations and games in this book have all been tested with elementary students, and found effective. Some have been used for several years. Complete directions are given. You need only make the ditto masters, and duplicating other simple materials will be greatly simplified by the book's special binding. I have included simulations and games on a variety of subjects to show how it can be done, as well as to make it easier for you to find subjects in which you have a special interest.

The direction each simulation takes will largely depend on you. You can use these simulations and games as starting points, and add or subtract as you desire. In many simulations, I have suggested extensions and variations. PANATINA (Chapter 3) can be presented in a hundred different versions, all easily tailored to a specific objective, the teacher's preference—and the needs of a specific classroom.

I have also included a chapter on simple ways to make your own simulations and games. Tailor-made simulations often work extremely well. You will find many "how-to's" to help you, as well as some things to do and some not to do and steps to take in designing a simulation game. There is also a chapter listing the major sources of other simulations and games and the names of some of the better ones I have used. I am including those I have used in my classroom and found effective.

So if you have heard about the use of simulations and games in the classroom, if you have never tried to use them but are curious about how they work, or if you have tried a few and would like more, here is the book for you. The simulations and games will make your day far more interesting because your students will discover they offer a provocative, exciting way to learn many of the things you are trying to teach them.

Jay W. Reese

Table of Contents

Simulations and games compared.
Why use them?
"An Inventory of Hunches."
Research—mine and other.
Further suggestions and ideas.

Role-playing, the oldest type of simulation.
How it differs from play-acting.
Tips on making role-playing effective.
Positive results of role-playing.

An example of beginning role-playing:
STRAWBERRY FARM* (29)

An example of open-ended role-playing:
ANDESIA (31)

An example of partially structured roles:
CENTRAL AMERICAN SUMMIT (38)

An example of fully structured roles:
INDIAN TREATY (41)

---

*Titles given in capital letters within a chapter are original games and simulations which will be presented in entirety for teacher to use in the classroom.

Other curriculum areas can be taught by using
   simulations and games.
Computer simulations.

An example of a simulation using mapwork:
   VOYAGEURS   (185)

An example of a simulation in teaching history:
   SPICE TRADE   (190)

An example of a simulation in class interaction:
   INFLUENCE   (197)

It's not hard to make your own; here's why.
Play some first.
Advantages of making your own simulations and games.
Re-design some existing games. Do variations,
How one of my simulations (REPORTERS) was developed.
Steps to follow in making your own simulation or game.
Some "Do's" in making your own simulation or game.
Some "Don'ts" in making your own simulation or game.
Why not develop one with your class? Do a "game game."
Developing simulations and games for the market.

Some good simulations I have used in the classroom and
   where to get them.
Some good board games and card games I have used and
   where to get them.
Good sources of new simulations and games: game
   publishers and dealers.

Simulation Games
and Learning Activities Kit
for the Elementary School

CHAPTER 1

How to Use Simulations and Games for Improved Learning

What are simulations? I know what games are. How do simulations resemble games? How do they differ from games?

Simulations and Games Compared.

The easiest way to define simulations is to compare them with games. Everyone knows what games are: there are sports games (hockey, soccer, basketball, golf, horseshoes); board games (checkers, chess, *Monopoly*); party games (Pin the Tail on the Donkey); children's games (hopscotch, hide and seek); and many others. The common elements to all of them are *rules* and *winners*.

Rules. Like games, simulations have rules. In a few simulations, the players make up rules as they go, but for the most part the rules are presented in manuals and instructions. As in games, players have to obey the rules in order to play the simulation (though there are exceptions).

Winners. Unlike games, simulations may or may not have winners. Many simulations do have winning individuals or teams, but just as many do not. In some simulations, the entire class may win or lose. The motive of "playing to win" may be less important in simulations than in games.

Other Comparisons.

Another difference between simulations and games is that simulations try to resemble certain aspects of "real life." Many games use symbolic playing pieces; chess, for example, has knights, bishops, kings, and queens. But most games (almost all of the sports games) are not designed to represent any facet of "real life," except indirectly. Some of the board games on the market today, like *Monopoly, Life, Careers,* and war games, do have a similarity to life situations, and thus they are a type of simulation.

Simulations are directly designed to teach, to live, certain aspects of life situations.

Some authors have tried to make very rigid definitions of a "game" as opposed to a "simulation" and a "simulation game." See some of the books in the bibliography.

Why Use Them?

The questions a pragmatic teacher will ask are "What are the advantages of using a simulation or game in the classroom?" and "Will students learn more, or learn faster?"

To reply to the first question, I am quoting from "An Inventory of Hunches":[1]

An Inventory of Hunches About Simulations as Educational Tools

1. Maybe simulations are "motivators." Their main payoff may be that they generate enthusiasm for or commitment to: (a) learning in general, (b) social studies or some other subject area, (c) a specific discipline like history, (d) a specific course, or (e) a specific teacher.

2. Maybe a simulation experience leads students to more sophisticated and relevant inquiry. That is, perhaps the important thing is what happens after the simulation is over, when students ask about the "model" which determined some of the elements of the simulation, about real world analogues to events and factors in the simulation, about processes like communication, about ways of dealing with stress and tension . . .

3. Maybe simulations give participants a more integrated view of the ways of men . . .

4. Maybe participants in simulations learn skills: decision-making, resource allocation, communication, persuasion, influence-resisting. Or maybe they learn how important these processes are. Maybe they learn about the rational and emotional components of these skills.

5. Maybe simulations affect attitudes: (a) maybe participants gain empathy for real-life decision-makers; (b) maybe they get a feeling that life is much more complicated than they ever imagined; (c) maybe they get a feeling they can do something important about affecting their personal life or the nation or the world.

---

[1]"An inventory of Hunches. Simulations as Educational Tools." Published by SIMILE II, P.O. Box 910, Del Mar, CA 92014. By permission of Dr. R. Garry Shirts, Director.

6. Maybe simulations provide participants with explicit, experiential, gut-level referents about ideas, concepts, and words used to describe human behavior . . . Maybe people know many things they don't know they know, and simulations act as an information retrieval device to help bring this knowledge to consciousness.

7. Maybe participants in simulations learn the form and content of the model which lies behind the simulation . . .

8. Maybe the main importance of simulations is their effect on the social setting in which learning takes place. Maybe their physical format alone, which demands a significant departure from the usual setup of a classroom (chair shuffling, grouping, possibly room dividers, etc.) produces a more relaxed, natural exchange between teacher and students later on . . . Maybe simulations' main payoff is that they create student enthusiasm in one classroom which may spread to informal student channels throughout the school.

9. Maybe simulations lead to personal growth. The high degree of involvement may provide . . . a better sense of how one appears to others; discovery of personal skills, abilities, fears, weaknesses, that weren't apparent before; opportunities to express affection, anger, and indifference without permanently crippling consequences.

Other Advantages.

Another advantage of using simulations is that they may cross subject lines. Elementary schools are so compartmented into the various school subjects that students seldom get a chance to use the skills and knowledge of one subject in another. Junior high schools are even more compartmented. It seems to me that at some time during the day, students should have a course in which the subjects are integrated.

Most of the simulations listed in this book cover more than one subject, even though I have included them in different chapter headings. An index by subject is included at the end.

Research—Mine.

Going on into the question of how well simulations teach, I'll give research examples. I was privileged one spring to do a pilot project under the Teacher Incentive Program (Title III). I used simulations and games to brighten interest in career education. The board games I used were BUSINESS MANAGEMENT, CAREERS, AIRPORT, LIFE, and ULCERS. The simulations I used were COUNCIL, DESIGN, MERCHANT, POLICE PATROL, REAL ESTATE, and

WHEATACRES. I also designed two more—a board game, CONSTRUCTION JOBS, and a simulation, SALESPERSONS (given in this book).

For three simulations (COUNCIL, DESIGN, and MERCHANT) I did a pre-test and a post-test with the classes. The average gain on the test was 13% (55% to 68%), and 79% of the students showed a gain.

For five simulations (MERCHANT, POLICE PATROL, REAL ESTATE, SALESPERSONS, and WHEATACRES), students were asked to list the typical problems found in the career, for each game. 87% of the students were able to list five or more.

For seven simulations (COUNCIL, DESIGN, POLICE PATROL, REAL ESTATE, CONSTRUCTION JOBS, SALESPERSONS, and WHEATACRES), students were asked two questions. 82% responded "Yes" to the question "Did this game help you understand the decisions made in this career?" and 81% responded "Yes" to the question "Should this game be played with next year's students?"

Three questions were asked of the students about the entire project. They responded as follows:

	Very little	Some		A great deal	
	1	2	3	4	5
How much did you learn from this project?	1%	2%	13%	30%	54%
How much did you enjoy this project?	5%	7%	14%	18%	56%

	No	Uncertain			Yes
	1	2	3	4	5
Do you think this project should be continued?	6%	2%	8%	7%	77%

There were about a hundred fifth and sixth grade students who participated, in four classes. Our school has a high turnover, so not all of the students who answered in the survey above had had all of the simulations.

In an effort to compare with students who had been taught career education in the traditional way, a control group was used, in another school. Students in both groups were asked to rate their school subjects on a scale as to how interesting they were. Results for career education were:

	Very Interesting	Kind of Interesting	So-so	Not Interesting	I Hate It
	1	2	3	4	5
Expermental Group	47%	33%	18%	2%	None
Control Group	23%	15%	38%	17%	6%

Though the results may not be scientifically significant, to me they show that the experiment was a success. (If you wish to see more of the statistics, they are included in Appendix 1.)

Other Research.

There is no published research as yet that proves the use of simulation games in the classroom gives students greater learnings than are achieved by those who have not used them. Of course, many of the advantages claimed for simulations cannot easily be measured. Also, the simulations upon which the various studies are based differ a great deal. Some of the studies with elementary students seem to show that there is a greater amount learned during a simulation game than by other methods of teaching. Also, a study with underachieving boys seems to show that they were able to focus and integrate other material better as a result of using simulation games.

For those who are interested in the actual research, a good summary is in a booklet by Chapman, Davis, and Meier.[2]

Suggestions on Choosing Players.

In the "Getting ready" or "To play" portions of the simulations in this book, I have suggested that students be chosen for various roles or positions, but have not suggested how they should be chosen. For a teacher who might want some ideas, here they are: (1) draw names from among those who volunteer; (2) draw names at random from the entire class, whether they volunteer or not; (3) ask the class to nominate students for the key positions and then either elect them by

---

[2]Chapman, Katherine; Davis, James E.; and Meier, Andrea. *Simulation/Games in Social Studies: What Do We Know?* Boulder, Colo.: Social Science Educational Consortium. 1974.

class ballot or choose them by lot; (4) number the roles or positions and ask the students to choose a number without knowing what the position is; or (5) choose the students outright. I have tried all of these and they all work.

Debriefing/Review/Discussion

One of the most important parts of any simulation game is the debriefing or review at the end. Many experts say that debriefing is *the* most important step.[3] After the game is over, students need to participate in a class discussion of what they have learned and the actions that were taken (and why), in order to verbalize what they have experienced. They can thus reflect on what they have learned, and discover how others felt about various parts of the game.

Spontaneous Discussion. I have had classes in which such debriefing discussions were spontaneous, in small groups, as they went to lunch or another class. This is the best kind, but of course not all of the students are able to participate or listen.

Directed Discussion. Teacher-directed discussions can serve very effectively. In each of the simulations given here, I have listed possible discussion questions. You may want to use other questions arising from your observations of class actions. Open-ended questions work best. Be sure to allow plenty of time for discussion after a simulation, but chop it off if the students lose interest.

How soon? Experts disagree as to whether it is better to hold debriefing discussions immediately after the simulation ends, or a day or so afterward. I have done both, and really don't see much difference. It depends upon schedules, time of day, and your own inclinations.

Don't ignore it. Mainly, don't ignore the debriefing discussion, or omit it. It is valuable and productive.
Evaluations/Tests.

Some simulation games on the market include pre- and post-tests to be given. Others don't. I have not included tests, as such, in this book. But you may use the questions listed in the debriefing sections as test questions if you wish.

---

[3]Note for instance the title of this article, "It's Not How You Play the Game . . . It's Whether You Talk About It Afterwards," by Clarice Stoll. *Media φ Methods.* January, 1972, p. 24 ff.

Assignments.

In most of the simulations in this book, I have included a section entitled "Assignments." You may use these or not as you wish. Some students will be motivated to do further work. You may also want to use these suggestions as homework assignments. The assignments give students a chance to use their research and writing skills, and to discover more about the topic.

CHAPTER 2

How to Use Role-Playing to Excite Student Interest

Role-playing is one of the oldest types of simulation. Good teachers have used spontaneous role-playing situations (impromptu dramas) for many years—and are still using them.

How Role-Playing Differs from Acting.

In a play, the words are to be memorized, and the actions are strictly dependent upon the scene. Theater acting requires rehearsal. Role-playing does not. Role-playing requires that the player enter into the thoughts and feelings of the person he is representing, so that the player can use his own words and actions.

How Role-Playing Has Been Used.

Role-playing has been used in schools to dramatize incidents in children's literature ("Pretend you are Pooh talking to Eeyore about his birthday"), to clarify thoughts and feelings ("Can you act out how you feel when Charles teases you?"), and to bring to life historical situations (Paul Revere's ride). In these cases, students were usually given a minimum of direction, and then allowed to develop their roles as they wished.

Role-playing is hard. Even though role-playing has been used for so many years, I found it harder to do than other simulations or games. Students of elementary and junior high ages need practice in role-playing, or they will portray totally unrealistic situations.

How to Make Role-Playing Easier.

Go slow on role-playing, especially if students have not had any practice in it. If this type of simulation does not work at first, don't lose heart. The next time you try it will be better. Some suggestions to make role-playing easier are (1) use creative drama first, (2) use an audio or video tape recorder, (3) discuss or simplify the roles, and (4) let students write summaries of their roles.

Creative drama. Some of the newer language arts textbooks have suggestions for creative drama, in which students play roles and act in spontaneous situations. This type of background is helpful in role-playing simulations. In one of my classes in which I used creative drama in language arts, the students were much more able to go into role-playing simulation, with a minimum of fuss and direction.

Tape recorders. In one of the role-playing simulations I did recently, I found that one class (of intelligent but not too self-reliant fifth graders) could not carry it off. One of the boys in particular created a role that was so unrealistic that it provoked laughter from the class, and the role situation fell flat. He said he was 95, had a family of twenty children, had been married seven times, and so on. (Come to think of it, he probably used this role to gain attention.)

So I taped one of the next role-playing sessions with the closed circuit television cameras and recorder from our district. I then replayed it. The class observed themselves in action, and without my having to lecture or point out mistakes, their role-playing improved. An audio tape recorder could have been used as well.

Discussion. In a role-playing simulation, don't be afraid to call time out if the roles are not going well, and lead the class in a discussion. Perhaps they don't understand their roles. Perhaps the role situation is beyond their experience, and needs to be simplified or reframed. If this is the case, feel free to do so. The class can help. Role-playing simulations, or any simulations, are not finished products. You need to tailor them to fit your class.

Summaries. Another way to improve role-playing is to give students a simple outline to fill out on paper. They may choose a name and an age for themselves, list what they have to say, and summarize their feelings as the role suggests. They put the role into their own terms and language in this summary. This makes the role more concrete and believable.

Positive Results of Role-Playing.

One of the positive results from the use of role-playing is what can happen to shy and quiet students. I recall one quiet sixth-grade girl who had a role that forced her to speak out, and to demand that certain things be done (see Role L5 in ANDESIA). She did a beautiful job; she was no longer Linda, the shy girl, but a strong person who had something to say and said it with force.

Some shy students can become absorbed in roles where they do not feel threatened, where they can take on the guise of another person. I was shy as a youngster, and the only time I came out of my shell was when I was acting out a role.

Another positive result is the development of empathy. Students who put themselves into the role of a poor farm laborer (as in ANDESIA) can begin to feel what a real farm laborer feels. Putting yourself into another person's shoes, another person's life situation, is one of the best ways to understand that person, and why he acts as he does.

The Simulations in This Chapter.

I am including in this chapter examples of four different types of role-playing simulations.

STRAWBERRY FARM is a simple role-playing exercise included as an introduction to role-playing for classes that have had little experience in this medium. Use it if you think your class needs it. Students are strawberry farmers, strawberry plants, and pickers.

ANDESIA is very loosely structured. In this simulation, students assume roles of laborers, miners, city residents, land owners, mine owners, and government leaders of an imaginary South American nation. Students are given descriptions of their roles and then they work out their roles in an open-ended simulation. The simulation can develop in many ways, depending upon how students play their roles and interract within their group. It gives students an idea of how people live in the Andes nations of South America.

CENTRAL AMERICAN SUMMIT is more structured. Students are given roles of actual government leaders of Central American nations and Mexico and the United States, and are asked to act and react as these persons might do when discussing possible unification. The character and the motives of these persons are left to the students. This simulation gives students an idea of the problems and opportunities of Central American nations.

INDIAN TREATY is tightly structured. Students are given roles of actual historical persons and must work within these roles. They are told what to say and how to react. The result, even so, will depend upon the student role-players. They are Indians and whites at deliberations leading to the signing of an Indian treaty in the American West in the middle of the nineteenth century. When I used this with a small class, I found students entered into the roles readily, and took their roles seriously.

STRAWBERRY FARM

Resume. A simulation to introduce students to role-playing. Students assume roles of farmers, strawberry plants and pickers on a strawberry farm.

Grade levels. Third through sixth grades.

Teaching objectives. (1) To give a simple beginning experience in the art of role-playing. (2) To give an understanding of how a strawberry farm works.

Participation. For a classroom of 20 to 30 students.

Materials needed. Printed instructions for the role-players.

Background information needed. None.

Getting ready. (1) Assign roles to the students as follows:

One announcer.
Two farmers—a boy and a girl.
One plant seller.
Ten (more or less) strawberry plants.
Six (more or less) strawberry pickers.

(2) Give the role-players their printed instructions.

To Play. After students have read their roles, answer such questions as necessary. Assign locations for the farm, plant store, and pickers' homes. Then let the announcer begin reading, and other players enter and play their roles as called for.

Side coach the players as the simulation progresses. Encourage Sam and Matilda (the farmers) to talk to each other and the other players (except the strawberry plants). At the end, encourage Sam and Matilda to say what they feel about the berry harvest (i.e., "It's been a good year, Matilda. Our plants gave us lots of strawberries.").

Debriefing. Ask students how they felt about their different roles. Discuss any problems that have come up.

Further suggestions. This simulation should not take much time. You might want to do it again and change roles for variety. Remember, students have to learn the art of role-playing. Don't be too concerned if it doesn't work perfectly at first. After students master this simple simulation, they are ready for more complicated role-playing simulations.

Assignments. Students could do research on strawberry plants and how and where they grow.

ROLES FOR STRAWBERRY FARM

Announcer. You are the announcer for this exercise. Read the following aloud. Pause at the places noted to give the players time to do what you say.

There were once a farmer named Sam and his wife Matilda. Sam and Matilda were tired of raising wheat and corn. They decided to raise strawberries instead. So they went to a plant seller to buy some strawberry plants. *[Pause.]*

Then Sam and Matilda took the strawberry plants back to their farm. *[Pause.]*

Back home, Sam and Matilda carefully planted the strawberry plants in two neat rows. *[Pause.]*

Then they watered the plants. *[Pause.]*

They gave the plants fertilizer. *[Pause.]*

And they watered the plants again, pulled weeds, and watched the plants grow. *[Pause.]*

The plants began to blossom with white flowers. *[Pause.]*

These flowers turned to little green berries. *[Pause.]*

The berries grew and became luscious ripe red strawberries. *[Pause.]*

Sam and Matilda needed to have the berries picked, so they hired some pickers. *[Pause.]*

The pickers took trays and began to pick strawberries from the plants. The plants talked to each other, but of course the pickers didn't hear it. *[Pause.]*

When the pickers' trays were full of berries, they took them to Sam and Matilda who weighed them and gave the pickers new trays. *[Pause.]*

At the end, Sam and Matilda paid the pickers. And the pickers went home. *[Pause.]*

Sam and Matilda had a good crop and made some money from their berries. *[Pause.]*

The End.

Farmers. You are strawberry farmers named Sam and Matilda. You should act as the Announcer tells you to. You will buy some strawberry plants and take them to your farm and plant them. There you will care for them until the strawberries are ripe. Then you will hire some pickers to pick the berries, and pay them when they have finished.

Plant Seller. You sell shrubs and plants. When Sam and Matilda come to you, you should sell them the strawberry plants—be sure to collect the money.

Strawberry Plants. You are a strawberry plant. Sit on the floor near the seller, and when you are sold, go with the farmers to their farm. When you are planted, sit on the floor again. When your strawberries begin to grow, extend your arms. You may talk to the other plants, but not to the people. You might want to say how good it feels when you are watered, and how you feel when your berries are picked ("Ouch!").

Pickers. You are a strawberry picker. Pretend you have a tray to put the berries in, and pick them from the plants. (If the plants talk to each other, remember you can't hear them.) You may talk to the other pickers if you wish and tell them about the day (is it hot, or cold?), and about the berries you are picking. You may eat a few if you wish. When your tray is full, take it to the farmers. When the berries have all been picked, the farmers will pay you and you will go home.

ANDESIA

Resume. Students assume roles of laborers, miners, city residents, land owners, mine owners, and government leaders of an imaginary South American nation. They make group and individual decisions and take action.

Grade levels. Works best with fifth and sixth grades.

Teaching objectives. (1) To give an understanding of problems of certain Latin American nations. (2) To give these problems a human background and encourage empathy. (3) To give an opportunity for teamwork in making group decisions.

Participation. For about 20 to 30 students.

Materials needed. (1) Each student is provided with a copy of the directions for his role. (2) It is helpful (but not necessary) to have cards or sheets to be used by the groups in recording their decisions:

Group Name _____ Our group has decided to
_____
_____
Group members in favor   _____
Group members opposed   _____

Background information needed. If students have a knowledge of social, economic, and political conditions in the Andes nations, particularly Peru and Bolivia, the simulation would become more realistic. (See "Background Material on the Andes Nations" below.)

Getting ready. Decide upon the role for each student, and give each his instructions to study. There are roles calling for individual action (City Residents), and you may want to give these roles to some students who work best by themselves. There are other roles calling for group action. You may want to choose class leaders for the roles of President, Opposition Leader, and Lawyer.

To play. After students have studied their roles, let the Laborers group and the Miners group meet separately to determine group decisions. It helps if they can meet privately, but this is not necessary. The majority rules in making decisions in both groups.

Once either or both groups have decided upon an action, call the Mine Owners, Hacienda Owners, and Government groups to separate meetings to decide upon their reactions. (Note that in the Government group the advisors give opinions, but the President makes the final decision.)

City Residents have individual actions during this time.

While the Miners and Farm Laborers have roles that direct them toward forming unions and striking, or taking more drastic action, it is possible either or both groups will not act. Some teacher direction may be needed in this case, for if there is no action by these groups, the simulation stops.

If a strike is called by either group, further direction may be necessary to avoid a deadlock. Students may need to stop the simulation, look up means of arbitration, and then begin again.

Further, if a revolution is called, the simulation might need to be stopped for a common decision as to how much support there is for a revolt, where the support is coming from, and what its chances of success are. It may also be necessary to agree upon specific population percentages and related social and economic factors for Andesia. Once a chance factor of success has been decided, someone may have to roll a die (or dice) to see if the revolution succeeded or failed.

The simulation may end at any time. ANDESIA is open-ended in that there are no predictable results. The teacher needs to be flexible and resourceful. Once the simulation has ended, a class discussion of all aspects of the simulation would be profitable.

Debriefing. Use questions such as the following to stimulate class discussions:

1. How did your group arrive at its decision? Did you agree with the decision? Why or why not?
2. How did you feel as a role-player? Was your role an easy or hard one to play? Did you feel you understood it? What could have made it easier?
3. How did you feel about the final decision at the end of the simulation?
4. If you were to do ANDESIA again, what would you change in it?

Assignments.

1. Read about the living conditions of miners in the Andes nations, and write a report. Tell what the nations are doing to change the conditions.

2. Write a report about the large haciendas in South America. How did they begin? How do they treat their workers? Are living conditions changing?

3. Report on the types of mines in Bolivia, Peru, and other nations. What ores are mined? Where are the ores shipped?

BACKGROUND MATERIAL ON THE ANDES NATIONS

While race is not an issue in this simulation, in some Andes nations the different groups are actually separate races.

In Bolivia, Indian families live on small subsistance level farms. Indians also work in the mines under better living conditions than the farmers. Mestizos are mostly middle class, and wealthier than the Indians. Whites are the upper class, controlling most of the industry and almost all the politics.

In Chile, the large estates, called *fundos*, were owned by a few wealthy families. Tenant farmers called *inquilinos* worked on them.

In the 1960's the government began a land reform to break up these estates. The copper mines were owned by U.S. companies until 1971, when they were nationalized.

In Ecuador, whites (10% of the population) are the wealthiest and most powerful group. They own the haciendas and the banana and cacao plantations where the mestizos work. There are few mines in Ecuador.

In Peru, many mestizos work on big haciendas or plantations, though some own their own farms. Some Indians also work on the haciendas, and some in the mines. Wealthy whites own the coastal plantations, and mestizos the large mountain farms. Whites control the mines and the government.

ANDESIA GROUPS AND ROLES

Group I: Farm Laborers and Families. (A majority of three must agree upon any action taken.)

L 1—You are a poor farm laborer with no permanent job. You are employed only when the hacienda owners need extra help. You have no land of your own. You have only a subsistence income. You want land of your own, or a good permanent job, so that you can feed your family well.

L 2—You are a poor farm laborer with a small plot of land of your own, but you have only a subsistence income from it. You want more land and a larger income. You feel the large farm estates (haciendas) must be divided up to give more land to poor persons like yourself. Then you will have a sufficient income.

L 3—You are an inquilino, or tenant farmer, on a large hacienda. You have a fair living, but you would like to own land of your own some day. You can't save to buy land on your present wages. Hacienda owners need to raise wages.

L 4—You are a fairly well-educated foreman on a large hacienda. You get good wages. You think workers should stick together and form a farm workers union, and you will help if they want to do this, because you know the workers don't get paid enough right now.

L 5—You are the son or daughter of a farm laborer. Your family once worked on a hacienda, but when your father became too sick to work the owner threw your family out. Your father died. You are bit-ter and angry at the hacienda owners, and you want all the haciendas divided up. You would be in favor of a revolution if this is what is needed. Tell the others in your group what happened to your father. Demand strong action—a strike, or a revolution.

Group II: Miners and Families. (A majority of three must agree upon any action taken.)

M 1—You are a miner. You work very long hours for very little pay, deep in a mine with dangerous working conditions. You want more money and shorter working hours.

M 2—You are a miner's son or daughter. Your father was recently killed in a mining accident, and there was no insurance for your mother and family. You want better safety conditions as well as more money for miners, and you want the mine owners to pay you compensation for your father's death.

M 3—You are a mine foreman. You get good wages. You support the mining companies and oppose any action by the miners, because you might lose your good job. But if a strong miners union would guarantee you your job, you would join one.

M 4—You are a miner. You want the other miners to help you form a mine workers union, and demand higher pay, shorter hours, and safer working conditions. If the owners refuse this, you think the miners should strike.

M 5—You are a miner. You have seen many years of near-starvation, miners killed in accidents, and other miners fired because they wanted a union. You believe a union won't do any good any more. You think that the only thing that will help is a revolution and government ownership of the mines. Try to get the others to join you.

Group III: City Residents. (Individual action.)

CR 1—You are a banker. You don't care what the government, mine workers, or farm laborers do, as long as they don't start a revolution. A revolution would do more harm than good, and might destroy your bank. Write a letter to the President of Andesia, and say what you think about this.

CR 2—You are a lawyer. If the miners or farm laborers want legal advice, or if they want someone to negotiate for them, you will be glad to help, free of charge. Write each of these groups a note, telling them this. If they would like you to help them, do so.

CR 3—You are a rich merchant in the capital. You own three businesses and a number of buildings. You are afraid of a general strike, a revolution, or higher taxes, for they would all hurt your businesses. You helped support the President and gave him money to get him elected. Write a letter to the President, telling him how you feel.

CR 4—You are the Opposition Leader in the Andesia Congress. You would like to be President. You feel that with the support of the miners and farm laborers, you could win an election. You don't want the present government to do anything now; then the President would become unpopular and you would get in. Write to the miners and farm laborers telling them you sympathize with them, and suggest a general strike for better conditions. Also write a letter to the President of Andesia, suggesting he take time to think things over carefully before acting.

CR 5—You are a newspaper reporter. Your job is to write news about what happens in Andesia. You may interview anyone you wish, visit whatever group you wish, and take notes. Then write newspaper articles about each group's actions, or each interview.

Group IV: Hacienda Owners and Managers. (A majority of three must agree upon any decision.)

H 1—Your family has owned a large hacienda for generations. You enjoy your trips to the United States and Europe, your yacht, airplane, and mansions, and do not want to give them up. If you paid your laborers more, you would have to give something up. So you oppose higher wages.

H 2—As a land owner you work hard to keep your hacienda up, since it is a small one. You would like to pay your laborers more, but if you do, you think the other land owners would object. You are sympathetic to the laborers. Try to persuade the other hacienda owners to give higher wages.

H 3—You are a rich land owner. You oppose higher wages for your laborers. You gave a large amount of money to elect the President of Andesia, and you expect him or her to support you and the other land owners. Once your group makes a decision, write the President, telling him or her what you think should be done and saying that if the laborers strike, the army might be used to break the strike and the union.

H 4—You own a medium-sized hacienda. You are willing to give the workers a little more money, say ten percent, if they don't join a union or get too greedy.

H 5—You make a good living managing a large hacienda for an absentee owner who lives in Europe. You could lose your job if the haciendas were divided up by the government. You don't want anything to happen that will lead to this. As for higher wages, sometimes you are in favor, sometimes you are opposed.

Group V: Mine Owners, Families, and Managers. (A majority of three must agree upon any action.)

O 1—You own one of the two largest mines in Andesia. To pay the workers more, or to improve their working conditions, the money would have to come from your own profits. You are not willing to allow this. You oppose higher wages, but as a last resort you will give the miners more, if it is necessary to avoid a revolution.

O 2—You manage a mine for absentee owners living in the United States. They are interested in high profits. Any raise of miners' wages would mean less profits. Less profits might mean they would fire you as a manager, so you oppose any wage increases.

O 3—As the technical supervisor of a mine, a mine engineer, you aim for high production. You don't really care about politics or whether or not the owners make a lot of money. In fact, you would like to improve the living conditions and wages of the miners, for that would mean the miners would work harder and increase production.

O 4—You are a mine owner. You know that mining conditions are bad and that wages are too low. What you would like to see is more automated machinery. You could employ fewer miners but you could pay them more. You would allow a mine workers union if the union would not oppose automation.

O 5—You are a mine owner, but you really don't know much about mining. You inherited all the mining stock from your father. You haven't ever visited the mines. All you know is that you are paid a good amount of money each year from mine profits, and you want this to continue.

Group VI: Government. (Final decision by President; others advise.)

G 1—You are the President of Andesia. You were elected by the support of the large land owners and mine owners and you owe them some help. But you are are afraid of a revolution. You would like to do something to help the farm laborers and miners, but you do not want to anger the owners. You must make the final decision as to what the government will do in case of a major strike or a revolution, but before doing anything you must ask the advice of the others in the government.

G 2—You are Minister of Defense for Andesia. You must have more money for a larger army and more equipment, because you feel there is danger of a revolution. You should tell the President you guarantee a revolution will be crushed, if your army gets more money.

G 3—You are Minister of Interior for Andesia. Your department is in charge of mines and farms. You can recommend to the President what you think is best. Try to find out more about conditions by sitting in on the laborers' and miners' meetings. If they won't let you do that, then interview some of the individual laborers and miners and ask them about the working conditions. Then recommend to the President what you think he should do.

G 4—You are Minister of Police for Andesia, similar to the FBI. Your informers tell you that there are Communist agents among the miners and farm laborers, and that they are trying to start a revolution. Tell the President. Ask him what you should do. Should you arrest the Communist agents and leaders of the miners and laborers?

G 5—You are Minister of Treasury for Andesia. There is enough money in the treasury right now for current expenses, but not any left over. If the President wants to do something that will involve spending more money, he must raise taxes—and the rich people won't like it. Make certain the President knows this.

CENTRAL AMERICAN SUMMIT

Resume. As government leaders of Central American nations, plus Mexico and the United States, students meet in a "summit meeting" to discuss uniting into one nation, and other problems.

Level. Sixth through twelfth grades.

Participation. Whole class.

Teaching objectives. (1) To give students an understanding of some aspects of Central American international relations. (2) To give students an experience of the give and take of a political conference. (3) To give students an opportunity to speak with logic and persuasion.

Material and background information needed. *Materials:* None, except for optional cards or posters giving the names of each of the nations.

Background information: Since students will represent leaders of specific actual nations, each student should be knowledgeable about the nation he/she is representing. How much background research to require depends upon your preference and the maturity of the students.

It would also be helpful (but not essential) for students to know about the historical United Provinces of Central America (1823-1838), why it was formed, and why dissolved.

Getting ready. (1) Choose students to represent each of the six Central American nations (Costa Rica, Guatemala, Honduras, Nicaragua, Panama, El Salvador). Choose others to represent Mexico, the United States, and British Honduras (Belize). The number of students per nation will depend upon the size of the class. A suggestion would be to have a President, Minister/Secretary of State, and Ministers/Secretaries of Commerce and Finance.

(2) Also choose a secretary or historian.

(3) Newspaper reporters may also be chosen, to write news articles about the sessions.

(4) Arrange the desks or tables in a circle, somewhat as follows:

Costa Rica

El Salvador   Guatemala

Honduras   Nicaragua

Panama   Mexico

United   British
States   Honduras (Belize)

(5) Use of a tape recorder seems to help students to speak more clearly, "for the record."

To play. (1) Ask the President of Costa Rica to act as Chairman for the first session. (Each session, a new Chairperson will preside, in rotation by nation, alphabetically.) Pose the first question for consideration: "Shall the Central American nations be united into a United States of Central America?"

(2) Each national leader should have a chance to give his/her arguments for or against such a union. (The United States, Mexico, and British Honduras may express their opinions if asked.) There may be more than one session of this step. At the end, the Chairman should call for a vote, and only the six Central American nations should vote.

(3) If the decision is favored by all six Central American nations, the second session becomes the constitutional convention of the U.S.C.A. (The United States and Mexican leaders must decide

whether or not to recognize the new union.) The convention could choose a President and other leaders for the new nation, design a flag, choose the location for the capital, and discuss and act upon drafting a constitution.

(4) If the decision is favored by at least half of the six Central American nations (with contiguous borders), they only should participate in the constitutional convention.

(5) If the decision is not favorable, or after the new U.S.C.A. has been formed, call another summit meeting to discuss the following questions:

    (a) The market price of bananas has dropped to its lowest level in twenty years. What can be done?

    (b) What should be done about the Hondurian claim to British Honduras (Belize)?

    (c) What should be done about the Panamanian treaty with the U.S. in regard to the Panama Canal? (If the U.S.C.A. which has been formed includes Panama, the question could be: Does the Panamanian treaty with the U.S. about the Panama Canal still apply?)

(6) The meetings may result in other actions—coalitions, treaties, threats—and the teacher may have to be flexible in dealing with the situations that develop.

(7) The simulation may end whenever you or the class decides.

Debriefing. Critique questions might include these: How realistic were the sessions? Did anything develop that might have developed in a real summit meeting? How did the leaders feel when their views were not adopted? When they were adopted? What may have been done differently?

Assignments.

    1. Do research and report to the class about the familiar foods we get from Central America.

    2. The Mayas were the earliest civilization in Central America. Make a report on the Mayan civilization from articles in encyclopedias, *National Geographics,* and books from the library.

    3. What earthquake zone lies in Central America? Report on the earthquakes in that region.

    4. What is the Pan American Highway? Make a map showing its route through Central America.

    5. How and when was the Panama Canal built? Who owns the canal? Who operates it? How do the locks work? Make a report.

BACKGROUND ON THE UNITED PROVINCES OF CENTRAL AMERICA
AND
OTHER STEPS TOWARD CENTRAL AMERICAN UNITY

The Central American nations became free of Spanish rule in 1821. They decided to become part of Mexico in 1822. But the union with Mexico was not popular with the citizens and in 1823 they left Mexico and formed the United Provinces of Central America.

The United Provinces existed as a nation for fifteen years. The central government and the local governments could not agree on many issues (much like the States' Rights movement in the United States during these years). In 1838 the United Provinces began to fall apart as one by one the provinces became independent republics.

In 1921, a new attempt at union began as all the republics except Nicaragua and Panama united into the Republic of Central America. Again, rivalries and disagreements caused this new nation to break up in less than a year.

Gradual steps toward unity have since been taken. In 1923 an association called the Central American Union was formed. In 1960, the republics formed the Central American Common Market. In 1964, they set up the Central American Monetary Union. The Organization of Central American States was formed in 1965.

INDIAN TREATY

A role-playing simulation by Jay Reese © 1975.

Resume. Students assume roles of Indians and whites at the deliberations leading to the signing of a typical Indian treaty in the middle of the nineteenth century in the American West.

Level. Sixth through twelfth grades.

Teaching objectives. (1) To present the human elements in the signing of an Indian treaty. (2) To enable students to view both whites and Indians with empathy. (3) To enable students to "remake history."

Participation. Twelve or more students.

Materials and background information needed. *Materials:* (1) Xeroxed map of the general area, one copy for each participant (see Figure 2-1). (2) Dittoed roles for participants, one for each. (3) Dittoed background information for participants, one for each (optional).

Background information: This is a simulation that must be treated with sensitivity. Knowledge of the Indian viewpoint of land is neces-

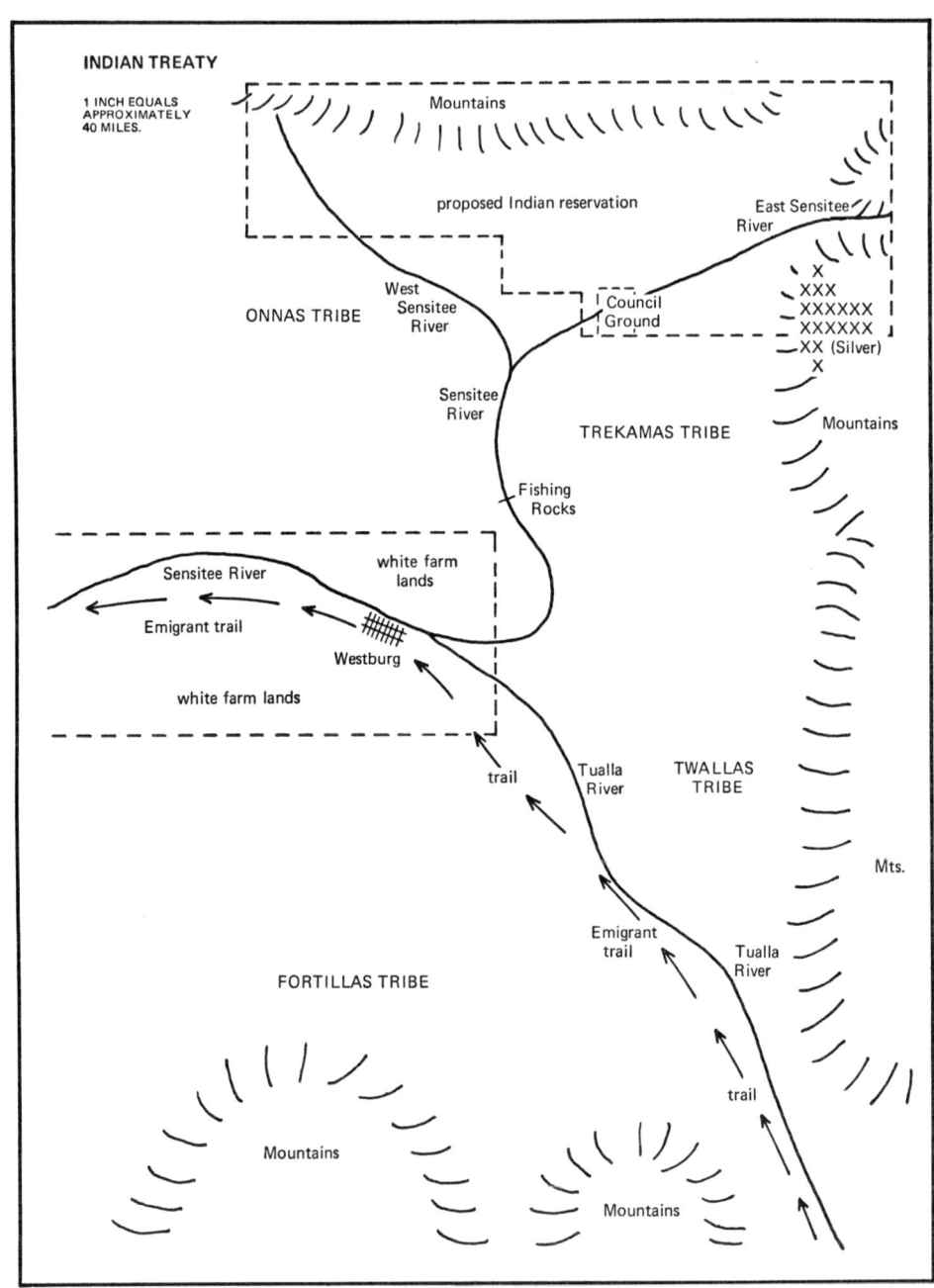

FIGURE 2-1: Map of General Area

sary for those who hold certain Indian roles. (See "Background Material on Indian Views of Land.")

The roles and incidents given here are based upon the historical Indian and white participants and events in the signing of an actual Indian treaty, though some extrapolation has been necessary. The historical treaty situation used was the Yakima Indian Treaty signed in June, 1855. The two influential Indian leaders of the signing of the Yakima treaty were Kamiakin, chief of the Yakimas (Meyakin in the simulation), and Peu-peu-mox-mox, chief of the Walla Wallas (Pumox in the simulation). The role of the woman interpreter was suggested by the role of Winema, a woman interpreter present at the negotiations trying to stave off the Modoc Indian War in 1873. Winema warned the whites of an Indian plot to kill them, and saved the lives of many.

BACKGROUND MATERIAL ON INDIAN VIEWS OF LAND

Most western Indian tribes viewed land with a semi-religious eye. Land contained religious spirits. Land could not be owned; therefore land could not be bought or sold. Many Indian leaders thought when they signed treaties they were giving a right to use the land or cross the land, and not the land itself. They did not realize they could no longer hunt or fish on the land just because of some marks on a paper.

By the 1850's, western Indians knew well what had happened to the eastern Indian tribes—how they had signed treaties, given up land, and how whites had broken the same treaties when they wished. The Indians knew most of the eastern tribes had been all but wiped out by war or white man's diseases. Western Indians were willing to go to war if necessary, even though they knew it was a war they could not win. But they wanted to keep their land as long as possible.

Getting ready. (1) Set the stage for the simulation by making available orally or by dittoes the information given under "To play."

(2) Assign the twelve roles. The whites are Steven Phillips, Jonathan Handlee, and George Sauce. The Indians are Five Feathers (Onnas tribe), Spotted Wolf (Onnas tribe), Pumox (Twallas tribe), Beyaire (Twallas tribe), Meyakin (Trekamas tribe), Sorhi (Trekamas tribe), Moccas (Fortillas tribe), Kolish (Fortillas tribe), and Tanema (woman interpreter). The four most important roles are Phillips, Handlee, Pumox, and Meyakin.

A secretary (recorder) is also necessary.

Other roles of soldiers, chiefs' wives, news reporters, and white townspeople could be assigned, though their roles might be mostly those of onlookers.

Option: This simulation could be presented as a play, an assembly program, or on television.

To play. (1) Place the role-players in a circle—in chairs or on the floor—for each session. Name tags help the role-players to know who the others are. Also helpful is a tape recorder, though this is not necessary.

For the first session, Phillips is in charge. He should tell of his plans to move the tribes to the reservation. He should then ask each chief or leader in turn to give his views on the treaty. After the first views have been exchanged, the first session ends.

(2) The second session begins with further role instructions to some of the participants. Discussion begins of yesterday's views and new developments. (Five Feathers warns Phillips of a plot and has moved to protect him. Phillips gives new inducements to the tribal leaders.)

(Use the third and later session instructions as you wish or as the simulation develops. Not all of them need be used.)

(3) The third session has further instructions to some role players: Handlee proposes a second reservation. Spotted Wolf arrives, and challenges Five Feathers for control of the Onnas tribe. (A historical note: At the signing of the Yakima Indian Treaty of 1855, war chief Looking Glass, age 70, arrived late in the sessions after a ride of three hundred miles in seven days. He challenged Chief Lawyer for control of the Nez Perce tribe. At a tribal council, Chief Lawyer's control was upheld.)

(4) The fourth session begins with Phillips giving fishing rights to Fishing Rocks to the Indians, together with an area of ten square miles around them. Five Feathers retains control of the Onnas. (Note: If you would rather make this control a matter of chance, you could give Spotted Wolf a one-in-six chance of winning, and roll a single die.)

It would be helpful for this and subsequent sessions if Phillips would present all of his proposals, together with any compromises he has worked out with the Indians, in writing, and begin to work out an actual written treaty, article by article. The role instructions do not mention this suggestion, but in classroom-testing this simulation, a written treaty which the whites and Indians could accept or reject or change, article by article, worked very well.

(5) The fifth session gives the last instructions to the role-players. It introduces the discovery of silver in the mountains. Part of the mines are in the proposed new reservation. (Historical note: Time is compressed here. In June, 1855, the Yakima Indian Treaty was signed. Soon after that, silver was discovered in Idaho. Miners crossing the Yakima Indian Reservation, plus white settlers who jumped the gun in settling before the treaty was ratified by the United States Senate, set off the Yakima Indian War of 1855-1856.)

(6) If everything else is settled, the sixth session could be the actual ceremony of the signing of the treaty. (See Figure 2-2.) Or there could be additional sessions until some agreement is reached.

If no agreement is reached, a war situation exists. This could lead to fruitful class discussions as to if and how it could have been averted.

Debriefing. Discuss with the class such questions as:

1. Did this simulation give you a better understanding of the Indians' side of wars?
2. Did this simulation give you a better understanding of the difficulties in making treaties with Indians?
3. Did the negotiations go the way you had hoped?
4. What would you do differently in this situation if you could?

Assignments.

1. Choose a group or tribe of Indians and make a report on their way of life.
2. Do research on Indians in your area—how they lived before the whites arrived, and what happened to them.
3. Read an Indian account of an Indian war or some other occurrence and report on it.
4. Try to reproduce some Indian art objects or other Indian gear for a display.

BACKGROUND INFORMATION FOR STUDENTS

(May be reproduced.)

Situation. An Indian Treaty Council.

Place. Traditional Indian council grounds in the Tualla valley in a United States territory somewhere in the Old West.

Time. May, sometime in the 1850's.

SAMPLE: Written Treaty.

TREATY BETWEEN THE UNITED STATES GOVERNMENT AND THE UNDER-SIGNED INDIAN TRIBES:

1. IT IS AGREED that the Onnas tribe and Trekamas tribe shall have a reservation of 1240 square miles on the north end of the valley, plus $200,000 cash per tribe.

2. IT IS AGREED that the Twallas tribe and Fortillas tribe shall have a reservation of one thousand square miles on the southeast end of the valley, plus $100,000 per tribe.

3. IT IS AGREED that each head chief of each tribe shall get $500 a year cash for twenty years, a furnished house, and ten acres of plowed and fenced land.

4. IT IS AGREED that each tribe shall be guaranteed rights to fish at Fishing Rocks and that no white persons shall be able to fish there.

5. IT IS AGREED that any tribal member may leave the reservation at any time and no restrictions shall be placed upon the movement of members of tribes.

6. IT IS AGREED that each member of each tribe shall be given a new blanket from the United States government.

7. OTHER SECTIONS MAY BE ADDED BY MUTUAL CONSENT.

8. THE UNITED STATES GOVERNMENT, WHEN THIS TREATY IS RATIFIED BY THE U.S. SENATE, GUARANTEES THESE RIGHTS TO THE TRIBES FOREVER.

SIGNED FOR THE UNITED STATES   SIGNED FOR THE TRIBES:
GOVERNMENT:

_____   _____
Steven Phillips, Head Indian Agent Meyakin, head chief of Trekamas

_____   _____
Jonathan Handlee, Indian Agent   Five Feathers, head chief of Onnas

WITNESSES:
                                    _____
                                    Pumox, head chief of Twallas

                                    _____
                                    Moccas, head chief of Fortillas

(Thanks to Art Fulcher for this page.)

FIGURE 2-2: Sample—Written Treaty

There are four major Indian tribes residing in the Tualla-Sensitee river valleys: the Fortillas, Onnas, Trekamas, and Twallas. The tribes total three thousand persons (counting women and children), divided approximately as follows: Onnas 1200, Twallas 500, Trekamas 1000, Fortillas 300.

An emigrant trail follows the Sensitee river, and at the joining of the Tualla and Sensitee rivers a white settlement called Westburg has begun. White farmlands surround the settlement for some eighty miles.

Indian Agent Steven Phillips (agent for the entire Territory) has called leaders of all the Indian tribes together to discuss moving the four tribes to a reservation on the northern end of the valley. The tribes have seen the whites settling in their valley and have been restless and hostile during the past few years, though there has been no war.

Phillips plans at least five sessions of the treaty council. He has brought beef cattle and a huge amount of potatoes, bacon, flour, coffee and sugar for the Indians at the council grounds. He has a guard of fifty U.S. Cavalry troopers. In addition, twenty-five white packers have helped haul the supplies in, and remain at the council grounds.

The two Indian leaders with the greatest influence among the tribes are Pumox, chief of the Twallas, and Meyakin, chief of the Trekamas.

No one can predict how the council session will end.

THE ROLES

First Session Instructions:

Steven Phillips. You are the Indian Superintendent for the Territory. You have called this meeting with the Indians upon instructions from Washington, D.C. You will be chairman of the sessions. You want all the tribes to move to a reservation of 1240 square miles on the north end of the valley. You are prepared to give the Onna tribe and the Trekama tribe $100,000 each for the land they are giving up, and the Twalla tribe and Fortilla tribe $50,000 each. You can, if you are pressed by the Indians, double these amounts. You can also promise each head chief $500 a year for twenty years, a furnished house, and ten acres of plowed and fenced land, though at first you will not mention this but will leave it as a later bargaining point. You can also promise the chiefs some personal goods such as blankets, food, and cattle, if you need to. You know, however, that this treaty must be ratified by the U.S. Senate, and if you promise more than the Senate will be willing to give, the treaty will not be ratified. So you must be realistic. Make certain the chiefs know they will not get the money you offer until the treaty is ratified by the "White Fathers" in Washington, D.C. Tell the Indians today about the reservation and then ask for their opinions. Just listen—don't comment. You may answer questions.

Jonathan Handlee. You are an Indian Agent and Assistant Superintendent for the Territory, and will be in charge of the reservation once the Indians sign the treaty. You are going along with Phillips' ideas about sending all the Indians to a reservation in the north end of the valley, but you are privately uncertain that the timing is right. You think it is too early to press the Indians very far. You are also sensitive to the Indians' views, and will want to push Phillips to accept some of their demands.

George Sauce. You are a leading merchant and Mayor of the local white settlement of Westburg. You represent the white settlers in the valley. You have no official voice in making the treaty, but if you are asked, you should tell the Indians that the white settlers want to be their friends and that the arrival of the whites in the valley is inevitable, and as sure as "the coming of winter." The Indians can do nothing to keep the whites from entering. They must accept the march of civilization.

Five Feathers. You are head chief of the Onnas, the largest tribe. You are at present friendly toward the whites, and willing to sign a treaty. But you have a rival for the leadership of the Onnas tribe, the war chief named Spotted Wolf. Fortunately he is not present now. He is extremely hostile to the whites and also wants to take over leadership of the tribe from you.

Spotted Wolf. You are war chief of the Onnas, the largest tribe, and you are planning to take over as head chief of the tribe, replacing Five Feathers. You are not present for the first or second sessions.

Pumox. You are head chief of the Twallas tribe. You have mixed emotions toward the whites. You want to be friendly, but you distrust them and are not sure they will keep their promises. Your view of land is similar to that held by all Indians: you feel land is something that cannot be sold or given away. It cannot be bartered for money or goods because goods and land are not equal. Goods are for using on the land. You do not understand how a white person can say he owns a portion of the land. You believe the Indians need more time to think over the matter of going to a reservation. You want a year's delay before deciding.

Beyaire. You are sub-chief of the Twallas tribe. You are friendly toward the whites and are in favor of the treaty. But you want to be certain the Indians have rights—guaranteed forever—to the use of the fishing place at Fishing Rocks, the common Indian fishing grounds where your people have fished for centuries. The whites need to be reminded about Fishing Rocks. You should ask for the right to continue fishing there.

Meyakin. You are head chief of the Trekamas tribe. You want peace between your people and the whites, but you are willing to go to war if you need to. You will not accept any white man's gifts, including the beef, bacon, potatoes, and coffee that Phillips has brought. You say that the Indians only want to be left alone in their own areas. You are not in favor of going to a reservation. But if it is the only thing that can be done, you plan to agree eventually (though you won't hint this, at the first session).

Sorhi. You are war chief of the Trekamas tribe. You are hostile toward the whites who have already taken some of the tribe's best grazing land for their farms and settlement. You are also bitter about the proposed reservation for it does not include Fishing Rocks, where the Indians of all tribes have gone for centuries to fish for salmon. You want the treaty to include a guarantee of Indian fishing rights at Fishing Rocks.

Moccas. You are head chief of the Fortillas tribe. You are friendly toward the whites, but you are unhappy at the prospect of losing all your tribal lands and having to go north to other lands with the other tribes. You want a separate reservation of your own, in your own traditional tribal area. You should mention this as a condition of signing the treaty.

Kolish. You are sub-chief of the Fortillas, under Moccas. You are leader of the younger men of your tribe. You are hostile toward the whites and will go to war if necessary. Indians, you feel, have no right to sell or give away their land that they have gotten from the Great Spirit. You are not in favor of a treaty or a reservation.

Tanema. You are the only woman present at the council meeting with an official standing. You are an interpreter. You are an Indian, daughter of Chief Old Feather, of a tribe far to the south. Your main objective is to avoid a war between the whites and the Indians, for you know that if there is a war the Indian women and children will suffer. You want the Indians to sign a treaty and live peacefully with the whites. If talk of war comes up, you should do your best to persuade the Indian leaders to accept the whites' terms and avoid bloodshed.

Second Session Instructions:

Five Feathers. Last night you overheard some young warriors talking about killing all the whites, particularly Phillips and Handlee. (You could not tell what tribe the warriors were from.) You warned Phillips of the threat and then moved your teepee and family into the whites' area to protect them. You do not want any bad incidents to destroy the meeting.

Phillips. Last night Five Feathers warned you of a plot by certain Indians to kill you and the other whites. He then moved his family into the white area to protect you. Today you will ignore this plot and won't mention it in the session unless someone brings it up. You are now ready to promise the tribes double the amount promised in the first session, namely that the Onnas and Trekamas will get $200,000 per tribe, and the Twallas and Fortillas $100,000 per tribe. Also you can promise the head chiefs the money and land stipulated in yesterday's session.

Handlee. Last night Five Feathers warned you and Phillips of a plot by certain Indians to kill you. He moved his family into the white area to protect you. You have your doubts as to whether there is really a plot, but you will say nothing about it today. (You think Five Feathers is using the plot to get more money for himself.) Phillips will promise the tribes more money today and you should urge the chiefs to accept.

Pumox. You have heard that Five Feathers warned Phillips and Handlee of an Indian plot to kill them. You are angry at Five Feathers because you yourself know of no plot, and you think he wants to get special privileges from the whites. Continue to emphasize what you said yesterday.

Meyakin. You have heard that Five Feathers warned Phillips and Handlee of an Indian plot to kill them. You are angry at Five Feathers because you know of no Indian plot and you think he wants more for himself and his tribe. You might suggest that the Indians meet privately by themselves today to talk this over and also to decide what you want to demand from the whites.

Moccas. You have heard that Five Feathers warned Phillips and Handlee of an Indian plot to kill them. You know of no Indian plot and wonder what Five Feathers is up to. Is he telling the truth or not?

Kolish. You have heard that Five Feathers warned Phillips and Handlee of an Indian plot to kill them. You know some of the younger braves in your tribe are actually plotting to kill the whites, but if the matter comes up today, you won't (to the whites, at least) admit you know anything. You may tell the Indians privately what you know.

(Other role-players continue with yesterday's instructions.)

Third Session Instructions:

Phillips. You will turn the chairmanship of the session over to Handlee today. He wants to introduce new concessions to the Indians, to which you have already agreed (mainly a second reservation on the southeast portion of the valley for the Twallas and Fortillas, with the first reservation in the north for the Onnas and Trekamas). You are also aware that Spotted Wolf has arrived, and that he is very hostile to the whites and wants war. He will now challenge Five Feathers for control of the Onnas tribe. The tribal council will be held this evening after this session ends. You privately wonder what this will do to the chances of the treaty, especially if Spotted Wolf wins control of the Onnas tribe. You are afraid it will mean war.

Handlee. You have Phillips' permission to introduce new concessions today. You will be chairman of today's session. You will promise that the first reservation (the one on the map) will be only for the Onnas and Trekamas tribes and that a second reservation of one thousand square miles will be provided on the southeast portion of the valley for the Twallas and Fortillas tribes. You will press the Indian leaders to agree to this.

Five Feathers. Last night, Spotted Wolf, war chief of your tribe, arrived after a long ride. He is fiercely against any settlement with the whites. He has asked that a tribal council of the Onnas tribe be held tonight after this session ends. There you are certain he will ask the tribe to choose between you (and your policy of cooperating with the whites) as the head chief. You do not know what your tribe will decide, so you cannot promise to agree to anything Phillips and Handlee bring up today.

Spotted Wolf. You arrived last night after a horseback ride of three hundred miles in seven days. You have asked that a council of your tribe, the Onnas, be held tonight after this session ends. There you will ask the tribe to choose between you (and your policy of Indian freedom from the whites) and Five Feathers (and his policy of appeasement to the whites) to be head chief. You are certain you will win. You are hostile and will talk against anything the whites say today. Tell the whites that you know they never keep their promises, so why should the Indians sign any paper? You have heard that other tribes in the East have signed treaties and then the whites have broken them.

Beyaire. If the whites have said nothing about Fishing Rocks so far, you will again ask Phillips to consider them. Insist that your tribe needs them.

Sorhi. If the whites have said nothing about Fishing Rocks so far, you will demand that Phillips give them to the Indians. Beyaire is also after the Fishing Rocks, so you two should work together.

Meyakin. Continue in your demands that the whites guarantee everything they say, and that there will be no broken treaties. You have heard that other tribes in the past have signed treaties, and then the whites have broken them. What guarantee can Phillips give that this one will not be broken?

(Other role-players continue with previous instructions.)

Fourth Session Instructions:

Phillips. You will make another concession today (if you have not done so previously), offering Fishing Rocks to the Indians forever. You hope this is the last concession you will have to make. You should urge the Indians to sign the treaty now. It would be helpful to have a written treaty ready to put before them giving all the provisions agreed upon (or presented), which they can sign today.

Handlee. Urge the Indians to sign the treaty today. Phillips is making his last concession. Remind the Indians that the whites and their civilization will continue to be here, no matter what they do. They might fight a war, but they would certainly lose. The whites have won every war with the Indians so far.

Sauce. You should continue to urge the Indians to sign a treaty, and to do it today.

Five Feathers. Last night the tribal council voted for you and your policies. Now that you know they are behind you, you can urge the other Indian leaders to sign the treaty.

Spotted Wolf. Last night the tribal council voted for Five Feathers and his policies. Your hope now is to get the other Indian leaders not to sign a treaty, but to resist the whites. Urge them to do so.

Pumox. Though you are still in favor of waiting a year before signing a treaty, you will follow Meyakin's lead today.

Meyakin. You still have not changed your distrust of the whites. Against all your feelings, you have decided to sign the treaty to prevent the outbreak of a war.

Kolish. You are still not certain the Indians have any right to sell or to give away their land. Land is not meant to be bought or sold.

Tanema. Ask the chiefs to sign the treaty today. Phillips has given them almost everything they want. Let the whites and the Indians live together in peace from now on.

Sorhi. You are still hostile to the whites, but if Meyakin signs the treaty, you will do so also.

Moccas. You are now in favor of signing the treaty.

Fifth Session Instructions (optional):

Phillips. You are aware that silver has been discovered in the mountains, and that part of the silver lode is in the proposed reservation. You will say nothing about it unless the Indians bring it up. Then agree to what you think is best.

Handlee. You are aware that silver has been discovered in the mountains and that part of the silver lode is in the proposed reservation in the north. You hope the Indians will say nothing about it, but if they bring the subject up, you can offer to exchange part of that land for other land in the west.

Meyakin. You have been told that silver has been discovered by white miners, and that part of the mines are in the proposed reservation for your tribe. Thousands of white miners are traveling there, you have been told, and many of them are crossing your proposed reservation. You demand that Phillips do something about this situation.

Five Feathers. You have been told that silver has been discovered in the mountains by white miners and that part of the mines are in the proposed reservation promised to your tribe. Thousands of white miners are traveling there and crossing your land, killing the game and trampling the grass. You demand that Phillips do something, or the Indians may go to war.

Spotted Wolf. You have been told that silver has been discovered in the mountains by white miners and that part of the mines are in the proposed reservation promised to your tribe. Thousands of white miners are traveling there and crossing reservation land, killing all of the game, and trampling the grass. This will give you a chance today to point out to the other Indian leaders that this proves the dishonesty and treachery of the whites. You should try to get the other chiefs to go war.

(Others continue with previous instructions.)

Supplementary information. Simulated roles and the actual persons they represent—

Steven Phillips—Governor Isaac Stevens of Washington Territory.
Jonathan Handlee—Assistant Indian Superintendent Joel Palmer, Washington Territory.
George Sauce—A typical white settler and merchant.

Five Feathers—Chief Lawyer, of the Nez Perce tribe.
Spotted Wolf—War Chief Looking Glass of the Nez Perce tribe.

Pumox—Chief Peu-peu-mox-mox of the Walla Walla tribe.
Beyaire—Chief Pierre of the Walla Walla tribe

Meyakin—Chief Kamiakin of the Yakima tribe.
Sorhi—Sub-chief Owhi of the Yakima tribe.

Moccas—Chief Sticcas of the Cayuse tribe.
Kolish—Chief Young Chief of the Cayuse tribe.

Tanema—Winema Riddle, Modoc interpreter of 1873.

Bibliography (specific):

Carey, Charles H. *A General History of Oregon.* Portland, Or.: Metropolitan Press. 1936. Volume II, pages 573 to 579.
Glassley, Ray H. *Pacific Northwest Indian Wars.* Portland, Or.: Binfords & Mort. 1953. Pages 110 and 111.

Bibliography (general background):

There are many good books giving general backgrounds of the thoughts, ideas, and feelings of the Indians during this period. Here are two samples:

Brown, Dee. *Bury My Heart at Wounded Knee.* New York, N.Y.: Holt, Rinehart, & Winston. 1970.
The World Book Encyclopedia. Chicago: Field Enterprises Corp. 1975. Volume 10, pages 108 to 139. ("Indian, American.")

CHAPTER 3

Simulations That Show How Governments Work

First Commercial Simulations.

When I first started planning simulations for my fifth and sixth grade students some years ago, there were few models to choose from. The high school and college simulations that had been published were almost all in the field of politics and international relations. There were DANGEROUS PARALLEL by Scott, Foreman, 1969; INTER-NATION SIMULATION by Science Research Associates, late 1960's; and CRISIS by Simile II, 1966.

So one of the first simulations I designed was PANATINA, given in full later in this chapter. Now, of course, many other simulations in the area of politics and government for elementary and junior high students have been published. Some of them are listed in Chapter 10.

Why Political Science Simulations?

Political science simulations are essential in grades four through nine because even at these levels students need to understand how governments work—all kinds of governments, from local school boards and city councils through county governments, state governments, national governments, and the United Nations. History and current events then become easier to understand. How could students understand the impeachment proceedings growing from Watergate if they did not know how our national constitution is set up?

Student Government.

One of the most rudimentary (and meaningful) governments for these grades is a classroom government and/or a student council government for the school. Many junior high schools have student councils. Not as many elementary schools do. Even if such a government has been set up, unless students can make real decisions, can see positive results of their deliberations, the structure is a farce. Giving student government any real power is hard to do, at least in the traditional schools. The more unstructured schools do it as a matter of course. Most classes are capable of running their own affairs, and drawing up a classroom constitution defining their powers. They can learn a great deal, even though the process of class meetings is time consuming.

Why Students Should Learn Self-Control.

If we want students who are independent, who can control their own behavior, can act in positive ways, then we need to give them practice in governing themselves. Students from strict authoritarian classrooms never learn the process of give and take, or the process of governing themselves, either individually or as a group.

A recent development for teachers is called "Teacher Effectiveness Training." The author of a book on the subject[1] makes it clear that children who learn self-control and decision-making from the earliest age become adults who are self-directive and can act without self-doubts. The converse is also true. Children who are constantly ordered, directed, and disciplined as they become adults find they cannot make up their own minds. I would recommend this book to all teachers who are interested in effective listening and in making "no-win, no-lose" decisions with their students. (In a "no-win, no-lose" decision, neither the teacher nor the student need be involved in a power struggle where one of the two wins and the other loses.)

Simulations in This Chapter.

In this chapter I am including two simulations that have to do with political science and decision-making at the governmental level. For understanding the actions of a local government, I recommend my published simulation COUNCIL, by *Interact* (see Chapter 10).

PANATINA is a simulation dealing with a national government. A president, vice president, cabinet, and congress must make decisions affecting a nation. Panatina is an imaginary nation in northern South America. Its leaders (students) are confronted with many problems which they must deal with as best they can. Sometimes

---

[1]Gordon, Dr. Thomas. *Teacher Effectiveness Training*. New York; Peter H. Wyden, Inc. 1974.

their decisions result in a change of government. The way the Panatina government works does not completely resemble the United States government, and in this way it introduces students to political science, comparing structures of government. Students also learn about the problems of a typical South American nation which has few natural resources to trade or bring wealth (at least in the beginning). PANATINA has proved itself a worth-while simulation.

BALANCE OF POWER goes into international relations in a simple way. It deals with interrelationships between national powers and the subject of influence and control of minor nations. Students work with a world map as leaders of four imaginary nations. They endeavor to keep peace while at the same time bringing as many small nations as possible under their influence. Students are thus able to see, in a simplified way, how the Cold War balance of power has worked.

PANATINA

Resume. As leaders of an imaginary South American nation, opposition, military, and private citizens, students deal with typical problems.

Teaching objectives. (1) To learn how national governments work. (2) To learn about problems of South America.

Participation. 17 (or more) students.

Time. Rounds of twenty minutes or more.

Grade levels. Sixth through ninth grades.

Getting ready. (1) Choose a historian who will keep the job straight through and write a "history" of Panatina as it occurs.

(2) Choose a President of Panatina. He/she will choose:

(a) Minister of State (Vice President)
(b) Minister of Defense
(c) Minister of Treasury
(d) other cabinet ministers if desired.

(3) Choose a Panatina general to represent the army command.
(4) Choose four Panatina senators to act as the Congress.
(5) Choose a President of the United States. He/she will choose:

(a) Secretary of Defense

  (b) Secretary of State
  (c) Secretary of Treasury.

To play. There are various decisions, called rounds (see following pages). First read the decision aloud and let the Panatina leaders (or whoever is mentioned) make their decision. If the decision involves the United States, then the U.S. leaders make their decision. It may involve a chance factor. Or the decision may involve the Panatina Congress. After the decision has been made, consult the "round" again—there is a list of possible decisions and possible outcomes of each decision. You should use these as suggestions. Other decisions not as obvious may be chosen, and you will have to use your own judgment in announcing the results.

  You need not use the decisions (rounds) in order, nor use them all. Choose what you want to present.

  You may use the background information as a dittoed hand-out, or read it to the class.

Extensions. In order to involve all the students, a number of middle-class positions could be added: airlines owner, banker, bus lines owner, cattle buyer, coffee buyer, department store owner, hotel and restaurant owner, import-export company owner, market owner, newspaper owner, radio station owner, small merchant, soccer club owner, and stockyards owner.

Debriefing. After the simulation has ended, lead the class in discussing such questions as:

  1. How did you feel in your position?
  2. Do you feel that some of your decisions were good ones?
  3. Are there some decisions you would have made differently?
  4. Did you feel you were a citizen of Panatina?
  5. What could have been done to make the simulation more realistic?

Assignments.

  1. Do research on one of the following nations, and give a report: Colombia, Venezuela, Guyana. Concentrate on the portion that might be in Panatina.
  2. Design a flag for Panatina.
  3. Design a coat of arms for Panatina.
  4. Draw a large bulletin-board map of Panatina.

5. Draw a large map of Panatina's capital city, and show places of interest (even your mansion, if you have one).

6. Devise a written constitution for Panatina, showing the powers and duties of the President and Congress.

7. Design and draw the capitol building for Panatina.

8. Make a relief map of Panatina from salt and flour, clay, plaster of Paris, or papier mache.

9. Draw a map of Panatina showing its roads, railroads, and airlines.

BACKGROUND INFORMATION ON PANATINA

Panatina is an imaginary nation in northern South America. It has the llanos area of Venezuela and Colombia, and part of the Andes Mountains. Its chief products are coffee and cattle. Cattle are mostly sold for beef and hides. It is a typical Latin American nation. The majority of the citizens are very poor, subsistence farmers.

How people live who earn less than $200 a year (most of the people in Panatina):

— Their furniture would be a few old blankets, a kitchen table, and one chair.

— Their clothing would be a worn dress or suit for each member of the family, and a shirt or blouse. There would be one pair of shoes, for the head of the family only.

— Food on hand would be a small bag of flour, some sugar and salt, a few moldy potatoes, a handful of onions, and a dish of fried beans.

— Their house would have no bathroom, no running water, no electricity.

— Their house would have only one room.

— There would be no reading material—no one can read.

— The nearest clinic or hospital would be ten miles away, with a midwife in charge.

— The cash on hand would be equal to about five U.S. dollars.

— The head of the family would have three tenant acres. On this he can grow $300 in cash crops a year, of which one-third goes to the landlord, and one-tenth to the moneylender.

— Life expectancy is reduced 25 to 30 years for each member of the family.

Round #1. To the President of Panatina: A revolution which started in the mountains is getting stronger. Your army is small and does not have modern arms or equipment. Your Minister of Defense says he cannot crush the revolution without more equipment, arms, and ammunition. Many people in the capital are becoming alarmed. The opposition leader says if you do nothing, he may have to take action to overthrow the government. What will you do?

Possible Choices:	*Possible Results:*
1. Appeal to the United States for aid.	1. Depends upon U.S. decision.
2. Appeal to the Org. of American States or the United Nations.	2. O.A.S. or U.N. do nothing but debate.
3. Do nothing; wait and see what happens.	3. Your government may be overthrown. Use Chance Factor below.
4. See if you can make a deal with the rebels.	4. Rebels ask to have a new person appointed as Minister of Defense. If this is done, rebellion ends.
5. Raise taxes and buy arms and equipment.	5. Must turn this matter over to Congress. See "Composition and Rules," below.

Chance Factors: Will the President of Panatina be overthrown or not? President must choose a number between one and six, inclusive. Results:

1. Nothing happens.
2. President is overthrown.*
3. Nothing happens.

4. Nothing happens.
5. Nothing happens.
6. President is overthrown.*

*If the President is overthrown, the former opposition leader in Congress becomes the new President and may appoint a new cabinet. Former President becomes opposition leader.

COMPOSITION AND RULES OF PANATINA CONGRESS AT BEGINNING OF SIMULATION

There are 102 votes. 52 are a majority. 75 are necessary to overthrow the President or pass over a veto.

The Panatina Congress has a parliamentary system, like England's.

The opposition leader has 35 votes.	(Players may vote all of
The rich landowner has 30 votes.	(
The llanero (ranch owner) has 30 votes.	(their votes in a bloc,
The subsistence farmer has 5 votes.	(
Army general has 1 vote.	(or split them.

(1 vote is reserved for teacher, in order to be able to introduce bills.)

The Vice President (Minister of State) is the chairman of Congress, but has no vote, except in case of a tie.

The President must approve all bills, or may veto them. If approved, they are a law; if vetoed, the Congress may pass them anyway, with 75 yes votes.

Members of Congress or the President may introduce bills.

Round #2. To the Panatina President:

Worldwide coffee prices have dropped drastically. Your treasury is almost empty. Since about half of the income of your people (and government) comes from coffee, that means depression. Unless something happens, many will starve. There may be a change of government, and you will be out of office. What will you do?

Possible Choices:	*Possible results:*
1. Do nothing; wait and see what happens.	1. President is overthrown; opposition leader becomes President.
2. Appeal to the U.S. to buy our coffee at a special price.	2. Depends upon action of U.S. President.
3. Appeal to the International Bank for a loan.	3. Your request for a loan was turned down.
4. Turn the matter over to Panatina Congress.	4. Depends upon Congress.

Round #3. To the Panatina President: Your Minister of Health reports that many of the poor people have no jobs, and are starving. Your minister of the Treasury says there is not enough money to support them on welfare (you have no welfare or social security now). Many may die unless you take action. What will you do?

Possible choices:	*Possible results:*
1. Do nothing; wait and see what happens.	1. Go on to the next round.
2. Appeal to the U.S. for aid.	2. Depends upon action of U.S. President.
3. Appeal to the International Bank for a loan for welfare.	3. Loan is turned down.
4. Appeal to UNICEF or the International Red Cross.	4. UNICEF or Red Cross are sending aid for starving families.
5. Turn the matter over to Congress. You must recommend a bill to be passed.	5. Depends upon Congress.

Round #4. To the Panatina President: The dreaded hoof and mouth disease has been found on the ranch of one of the senators of your party. Unless the disease is stopped, it will spread. The only way to stop it is to kill diseased cattle and burn them. You do not have enough money to handle the disease if it begins to spread. Will you pay the senator for the cattle, if they are killed? What will you do?

Possible choices:

1. Do nothing; wait and see what happens.

2. Appeal to the U.S. for money and help.
3. Appeal to the U.N. (Food & Agric. Org.) for aid.
4. Destroy the cattle on the senator's ranch.

5. Turn the matter over to Congress.

Possible results:

1. Your government is overthrown. Opposition leader becomes new President.

2. Depends upon action of U.S. President.
3. FAO help is sent. The disease is stopped.
4. Unless you pay the senator for the cattle destroyed, you will lose his support. How much will you pay?

5. Depends upon actions of Congress.

Round #5. To the Panatina President: Your Minister of Health reports that there has been a great increase in tropical diseases among the poor people—diseases like malaria, yaws, leprosy. You do not have enough doctors, hospitals, or medicines to help them. Many will die unless they get help. What will you do?

Possible choices:

1. Do nothing.
2. Appeal to the U.S. for a loan to build dams.
3. Appeal to the U.N. (Economic Commission for Lation America) for help to build dams.
4. Ask the International Bank for a loan to build dams.
5. Turn the matter over to Congress.

Possible results:

1. Go on to the next round.
2. Depends upon action of U.S. President.
3. E.C.L.A. sends a commission to study the situation. They may send you aid in five years.
4. International Bank will not give a loan at this time.
5. Depends upon action of Panatina Congress.

Round #6. To the Panatina President: Your nation has many good rivers which could be harnessed by dams for electric power and irrigation. Your Minister of Interior recommends dams be built because they would provide power for new industries and irrigation for new farms (the llanos are very dry). This would help your nation.

But you do not have enough money in the treasury to build dams. What will you do?

Possible choices:

1. Do nothing.
2. Appeal to the U.S. for a loan to build dams.
3. Appeal to the U.N. (Economic Commission for Latin America) for help to build dams.
4. Ask the International Bank for a loan to build dams.
5. Turn the matter over to Congress.

Possible results:

1. Go on to the next round.
2. Depends upon action of U.S. President.
3. E.C.L.A. sends a commission to study the situation. They may send you aid in five years.
4. International Bank will not give a loan at this time.
5. Depends upon action of Panatina Congress.

Round # 7. To the President of Panatina: Many persons in Panatina are asking for land reforms. Only about five thousand persons own 90% of the good farm land. They are very rich. The others own 10% of the land, or work for the rich landowners, or are unemployed. Unless you do something, there may be a revolution. But the rich landowners support your government. What will you do?

Possible choices:

1. Tell the rich landowners they must give up half their land. Twenty-year government bonds will be given to them in payment.
2. Turn the matter over to Congress.
3. Do nothing; wait and see what happens.

Possible results:

1. Rich landowners refuse. Go on to Round #8.

2. Depends upon action of Congress.
3. Choose a number between 1 and 6:

    (1) No revolution. (4) No revolution.
    (2) No revolution. (5) Revolt tried, but fails.
    (3) Revolt succeeds.*(6) No revolution.

*Opposition leader is new President. What will he do to solve the problem?

Round #8. To the President of Panatina: A group of people have come to see you. They represent the New Party, composed of poor persons in Panatina. They demand you do the following things: (1) Hold new elections for Congress, to be properly supervised, secret ballot. (2) See that at least half of the persons in the President's cabinet are from the New Party. (3) See that more land is given to the poor people. If these things are done, they will support you in the next election. What will you do?

Possible choices:

1. Do nothing; turn down their demands.
2. Turn the matter over to Congress.
3. Negotiate with the leader of the New Party.

4. Give in to the demands.

Possible results:

1. Go on to Round #9.

2. Depends upon action of Congress.

3. Leaders of the New Party will give up their second demand, if they can get numbers 1 and 3. If the president introduces a bill in Congress on land reform, this will suffice for number 3.

4. Go on to Round #9.

Round #9. To the President of Panatina: Elections are coming up in Panatina. You must choose whether to run for re-election as President or not. What will you do?

1. Choose not to run.

2. Choose to run again. If you do, choose a number between 1 and 6.

1. A new candidate for President is needed.

2. Results:

A. (If President turned New Party's demands over to Congress):

1. re-elected	4. re-elected
2. defeated	5. defeated
3. re-elected	6. re-elected

B. (If President ignored New Party's demands):

1. re-elected	4. re-elected
2. defeated	5. defeated
3. re-elected	6. defeated

C. (If President gave in to all or part of New Party's demands):

1. re-elected	4. re-elected
2. defeated	5. re-elected
3. re-elected	6. re-elected

Round #10. To the Panatina CONGRESS: The New Party has introduced the following bills:

1. Break up the large estates and give all the land to the poor people. How much to pay the landowners is up to Congress.
2. No one person is to own more than 250 hectares of land.
3. If Bill #2 does not pass, triple the property taxes on ranches larger than 250 hectares. If Bill #2 passes, this bill is withdrawn.

4. Have effective rent controls and a rent ceiling for tenant farmers.

5. Have effective lending controls and an interest ceiling.

What will Congress do?

Composition of Panatina Congress (more persons added), since last elections:

1. Opposition leader controls 15 votes.
2. New Party leader controls 25 votes.
3. Subsistence farmer controls 15 votes.
4. Poor laborer controls 15 votes.
5. Rich landowner controls 15 votes.
6. Middle class merchant controls 15 votes.
7. Army general has 1 vote.
(1 vote reserved for teacher.)

Possible choices:	*Possible results:*
Pass or reject each bill. If bills are passed, President must OK or veto them.	None suggested. Up to teacher.

Round # 11. To the President of Panatina: An important iron ore field has been discovered in the Pacaima Mountains. You need money to develop it. A United States company (the K-P Company) says it will develop the ore field and pay Panatina the value of 10% of the ore taken. A Russian company (the Kruchaya Company) says it will develop the ore field and build a steel mill in Panatina, and pay Panatina 10% of the profits of both. A Japanese company (the Obisan Company) will do the same as the Russians, except they will *guarantee* to pay 7% of the value of the ore and 5% of the sales of the steel mill. A European company (the Paris-Panatina Company) will do the same as the U.S. company, except they will pay 15% of the value of the ore taken. What will you do?

Possible choices:	*Possible results:*
1. Do nothing; wait and see.	1. A revolution is imminent. Teacher judgment.
2,3,4,5. Accept U.S., Russian, Japanese, or European offer.	2,3,4,5. Results will be seen later.
6. Reject all offers and make own terms.	6. Variable. Teacher judgment.

7. Go on our own; get a loan from International Bank and develop the ore field and build a steel mill.	7. Choose a number between 1 and 6: (1) Loan granted. (4) Loan turned down. (2) Loan turned down. (5) Loan turned down. (3) Loan turned down. (6) Loan turned down.

Round #12. To the President of Panatina: The government of Venezuela has invited the government of Panatina to join in talks leading to a South American Common Market. What will you do?

(Note: This may produce a need for research, to find out more about a common market, its advantages and disadvantages, before a decision is made.)

Possible choices:

Possible results:

1. Do nothing; do not join.

1. Panatina will lose money if the other nations join and you do not. Your government may be overthrown. (Teacher judgment.)

2. Join in talks about a Common Market.

2. Panatina will prosper. Your re-election is assured.

3. Ask the U.S. for advice.

3. Depends upon U.S. President.

4. Turn the matter over to Congress.

4. Depends upon Panatina Congress.

Round #13. To the President of Panatina: Some of the South American nations are discussing a conference in which the nations will unite in a United States of South America. What will you do?

Possible choices:

Possible results:

1. Do nothing; do not join.

1. Go on to the next round.

2. Join in a conference discussing the possible U.S.S.A.

2. This is a good chance for an extension of the simulation. The government of Panatina and other nations could be represented in the conference.

3. Ask the U.S. for advice.

3. Depends upon U.S. President.

4. Actively promote the U.S.S.A.

4. Assume the U.S.S.A. has been voted on. Can set up a Constitutional Convention for the new nation.

Round #14. To the President of Panatina: Your first payment on your iron ore has come in. To find out the amount, see below. How will you spend it?

Amount of payment:

1. If you accepted the K-P Company (U.S.) you get $30 million, U.S.
2. If you accepted the Kruchaya Company (Russian), you get 200,000 Panatina Pesos (worth $100,000 U.S.).
3. If you accepted the Obisan Company (Japanese), you get 14 million Panatina Pesos (worth $7 million U.S.).
4. If you accepted the Paris-Panatina Company (European), you get 72 million Panatina Pesos (worth $36 million U.S.).
5. If you made any other agreement, the amount will vary. Teacher judgment.

Possible choices and results:

The possible choices and results are almost infinite. Teacher judgment is needed.

BALANCE OF POWER

Resume. Students work with a world map as leaders of four imaginary nations. They endeavor to keep peace while at the same time bringing as many small nations as possible under their influence.

Teaching objectives: (1) To experience a Cold War balance of power between great world nations. (2) To develop strategies to maintain the balance of power.

Grade levels. Sixth through eighth grades.

Participation. Four to eight students, or four committees of students.

Materials necessary. (1) A map for bulletin board (Figure 3-1).
(2) Set of Action Cards (see listed in Figure 3-2).
(3) Tally chart (Figure 3-3).
(4) A single die or set of cards numbered one through six.

Getting ready. (1) Prepare the map, charts, and cards.
(2) Choose four or eight students to play, and one as recorder. If you wish, you can divide your class into four groups, with each group representing one nation.

To play. (1) Explain the rules to the students:

You are leaders of four great world nations on an imaginary planet. You must try to maintain a balance of power, and peace, by keeping each other from gaining at least three hundred "Power Factors." If one of the four nations gains at least three hundred Power Factors, the

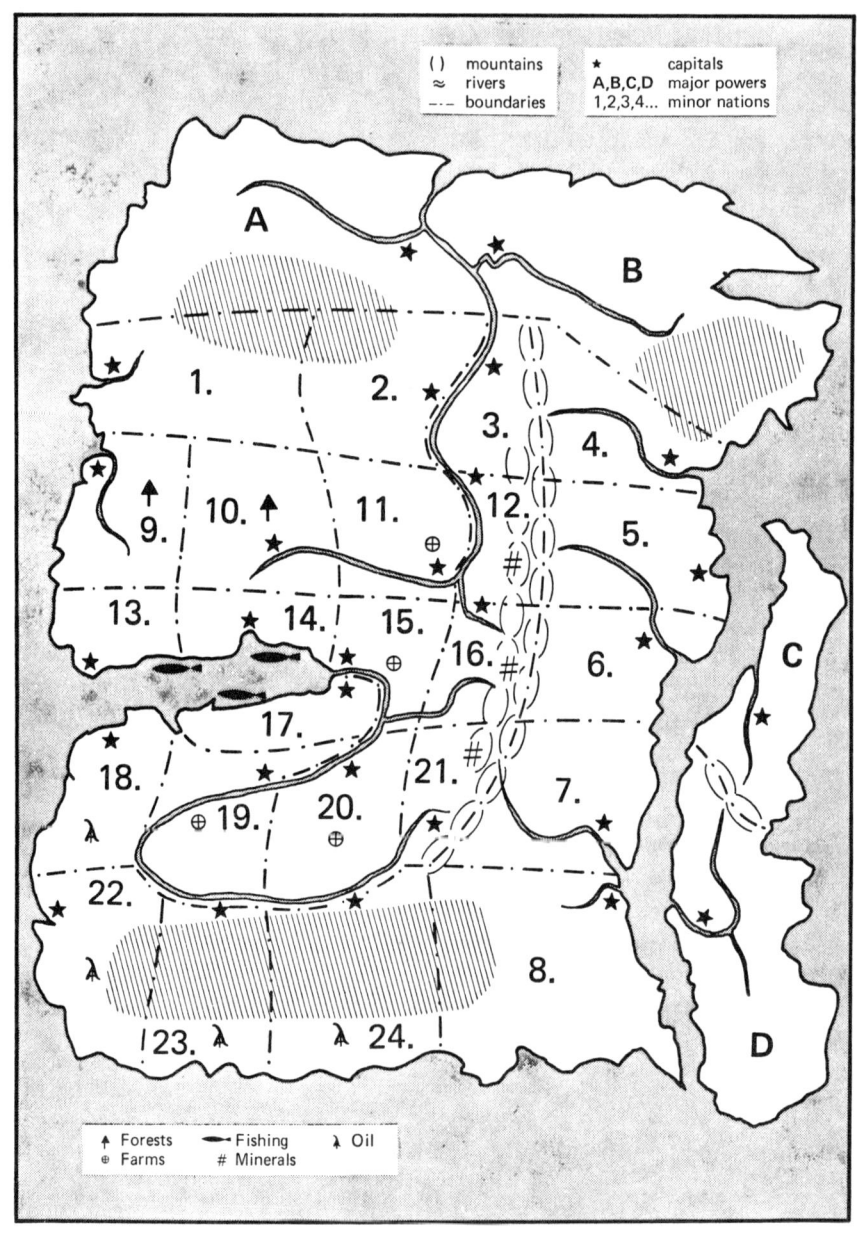

FIGURE 3-1: Map for Bulletin Board

BALANCE OF POWER—ACTION CARDS (Total of 24)

Four each:	Action—Foreign Aid is given to five nations.
	Gain three Power Factors in each of five small nations.
Four each:	Action—Loans are granted to three nations.
	Gain five Power Factors in each of three small nations.
Four each:	Action—Medical and Educational help is sent to seven nations.
	Gain two Power Factors in each of seven small nations.
Four each:	Action—Propaganda is used to tell other nations how great you are.
	Gain four Power Factors in each of four small nations.
Two each:	Action—A contract is given to buy oil.
	Gain fifteen Power Factors in one oil nation.
Two each:	Action—A contract is given to buy ore.
	Gain fifteen Power Factors in one mining nation.
Two each:	Action—Farm produce is bought from two nations.
	Gain seven Power Factors in two farming nations.
Two each:	Action—Contracts are given to buy lumber or fish.
	Gain five Power Factors in three lumber or fishing nations.

FIGURE 3-2: Action Cards (total of 24)

balance has been broken, and war will ensue. The nation with the three hundred Power Factors will most likely win and the other three lose, though in a nuclear war everyone loses, and probably none of the present leaders will survive.

The great powers cannot use military force. Treaties and alignment of small powers are done through social, economic, and propaganda forces.

The great powers begin with five Power Factors in each of the two small powers on their borders.

(2) On the first round, each national leader draws a card and acts upon it by deciding over which of the small powers to exert influence. Results are placed upon the chart.

(3) On the second and subsequent rounds, the national leaders may either draw a card or call a "Confrontation."

A Confrontation is used to gain an opponent's Power Factors in any one small nation. The challenger names the nation, and rolls a die or draws one of the numbered cards. (Challenger must have at least five Power Factors in that nation.)

	Power Factor	Factors Gained or Lost				Final Power Factors			
		A	B	C	D	A	B	C	D
Large Powers	50 ea.	50	50	50	50	50	50	50	50
Small Powers:									
1. (Borders A)	10	5							
2. (Borders A)	10	5							
3. (Borders B)	10		5						
4. (Borders B)	10		5						
5. (Borders C)	10			5					
6. (Borders C)	10			5					
7. (Borders D)	10				5				
8. (Borders D)	10				5				
9. (Timber)	20								
10. (Timber)	20								
11. (Farming)	30								
12. (Mines)	30								
13. (Fishing)	20								
14. (Fishing)	20								
15. (Farming)	30								
16. (Mines)	30								
17. (Fishing)	20								
18. (Oil)	40								
19. (Farming)	30								
20. (Farming)	30								
21. (Mines)	30								
22. (Oil)	40								
23. (Oil)	40								
24. (Oil)	40								
Total	550 (300 needed)								

FIGURE 3-3: Tally Chart

Results (number is from die or card):

1. Challenger gains Power Factors equal to his own, from opponent.
2. Challenger gains all opponent's Power Factors in that nation.
3. Challenger gains half opponent's Power Factors in that nation.
4. Challenger gains half opponent's Power Factors in that nation.
5. Challenger loses all of his Power Factors in that nation to his opponent.
6. No change.

(4) When one major power gains all the Power Factors in a small nation, the total is placed on the "Final" column of the tally sheet. No other major power can gain those Power Factors.

(5) There can be no more Power Factors than are listed for the nation. For instance, see Nation 10—no more than 20 Power Factors can be placed there.

(6) Game ends when one major power gains three hundred Power Factors, or when it is evident that a balance of power will remain.

Debriefing. Discuss strategies and how the game relates to the Cold War.

Extensions. This game could be set up as a board game for four students.

Assignments.

1. Draw a larger map of your own nation. Add as many details as you can.
2. Design a flag for your nation.
3. Tell what kind of government your nation has, and how it works. Give the name of the leaders.
4. Imagine a history of your nation and write it down.
5. Write what happens during the game as if you were a news reporter giving the latest news to persons in your nation.
6. Do research on terms like "Cold War" and "Balance of Power." Tell where and when these terms were used.
7. Give your nation a name. Name the capital, large cities, rivers, mountains, and other features. Draw a map showing these names.

CHAPTER **4**

Activities That Teach Economics

Why Bother with Economics?

"Students graduate from high school or college and then proceed to buy cars that do not run, pay interest rates that are exorbitant, undertake business ventures that fail . . . . The school experience clearly does not prepare students for their real-world roles as consumers, job-holders, savers and investors. Moreover, lack of down-to-earth familiarity with fundamental economic principles impairs their effectiveness as citizens sharing in political decisions that affect us all."[1]

What Causes Bad Economic Teaching?

"The situation just described is caused primarily by: (1) the notable absence of economics and economic concepts in most school curricula; (2) the woefully inadequate economics preparation of most teachers; and (3) the ineffective teaching of economics (when it does appear in the curriculum, and even when taught by teachers trained in economics)."[2]

Many classroom teachers are probably like I was—to me the idea of teaching economics sounded dull. And the reason is probably the same—a required college course in economics that was dry, boring, and filled with dusty theory. My economics class was a year long, and it certainly could not be understood by elementary and junior high students; I didn't understand some of it myself!

---

[1]Kourilsky, Marilyn. *Beyond Simulation.* Los Angeles: Educational Resource Associates, Inc. 1974, p. 1.

---

[2]*Ibid.*

What Is Economics?

Yet if we forget about college courses entitled "Principles of Economics I" and think for a moment what the subject really covers, I am sure attitudes will change.

Economics (as far as elementary, junior high students are concerned) covers all of the everyday life that deals with money, with banks, with taxes, with earning, saving, and spending, with our total capitalistic free enterprise system. Topics such as inflation, depression, recession, partnerships, corporations, cooperatives, and trade are a few that can be taught by using simulations.

Importance. And if we take the large view of economics just mentioned, we can see how important it is for students to learn about economics. Why wait until senior high school to give students experience in writing checks and balancing checkbooks? Students in elementary and junior high grades are earning money—and spending it. Why not give them an experience in saving it, and letting it earn interest? I could go on and on.

Monopoly.

The enduring popularity of a board game, *Monopoly,* shows that people like to deal with the subject of money. It, the game, is a beginning in giving players a chance to learn about real estate, rentals, interest, taxes, and investments. Students who have not played this game (and there are a few) should have the opportunity to play it or others like it.

The Mini-Economy.

Another good way of bringing practical economics to life in the classroom is by means of the "mini-economy." In a mini-economy, students have their own money, spend it, start classroom businesses, do banking, and can branch out into many other enterprises. For those who are interested in finding out more about this type of simulation, see the book I just quoted from, *Beyond Simulation,* by Dr. Marilyn Kourilsky.

Simulations in This Chapter.

The best way to teach economics is to start by using simulations. In this chapter I am enclosing directions for four simulations involving various aspects of economics: BLUE WODJET COMPANY, LAN-DOSA, GALACTICA, and CLASSROOM STOCK MARKET.

BLUE WODJET COMPANY is a simulation dealing with corporations and how they are run. Students are stockholders, managers, and personnel of an imaginary manufacturing concern. Others are residents of the city where the company is located. Each participates as his role requires.

LANDOSA deals with runaway inflation. It is unique in that students do not at first realize this is the aim of the game. All they know is that they are dealing with farms and profits in an imaginary nation. Then they realize what inflation is doing, and they have to see if they can stop it.

GALACTICA deals with trade and the free enterprise system. Students are traders from various planets with specialized goods to trade and specific goods to obtain. It also goes into the money system and what makes money valuable. I found it a good simulation to use in starting a class year—giving students a chance to interact with each other and get acquainted.

CLASSROOM STOCK MARKET deals with shares of stock, stock exchanges, and stock values. Students buy stocks in corporations formed with *Monopoly* properties, elect officers, and collect dividends. A stock market board lists stocks and market values. Since most students have played *Monopoly,* it takes a minimum of explanation.

THE BLUE WODJET COMPANY
A simulation by Jay Reese

Resume. Students are stockholders, managers, and personnel of an imaginary manufacturing concern. Others are residents of the city where this company is located. Each participates as his role requires.

Grade levels. Sixth through tenth graders.

Participants. 25 to 30 students.

Teaching objectives. (1) To give an understanding of corporate structure. (2) To develop an understanding of industrial problems. (3) To stimulate an awareness of the industrial side of pollution problems. (4) To give an understanding of a profit and loss statement. (5) To give an understanding of the process of wage and salary negotiations.

Materials and background information needed. *Materials.* (1) Dittoed copies of Form 1, one per participant.

(2) Dittoed copies of Form 2, one per student as needed.

(3) Dittoed copies of Form 3, one per student as needed.

Background information: Some practice in filling out a profit and loss statement may be helpful before starting the simulation.

Students may ask, "What is a wodjet?" A wodjet can be anything you want it to be. One description is that it is a vital part of a non-polluting steam automobile engine of the 1980's.

Getting ready. (1) Teacher or leader must choose five to ten stockholders, each to own one hundred shares in the Blue Wodjet Company.

(2) Stockholders then meet and elect a Chairman of the Board, and also choose a company president, preferably from the rest of the class.

(3) Company president chooses the company officers: Advertising Manager, Personnel Manager, Sales Manager, Production Manager, Treasurer, and Vice President (six persons).

(4) Personnel manager "hires" six to eight workers and two foremen, and sets their pay scale according to the earning schedule (Form 3). Two workers are to be at Level #1, two or three at Level #2, and the others at Level #3. Foremen are at Level #4.

(5) Teacher or leader chooses townspeople from the remaining members of the class. (If necessary, some of them can be stockholders also.) The list of townspeople could include auto sales owner, banker, department store owner, mayor, newspaper owner, and real estate owner. (There can be more than one student in each position, except that of mayor.)

To play. (1) Distribute the forms to the participants.

(2) Explain how to fill out the forms.

(3) Read aloud the first decision to the company president and the officers. (The rest of the class may listen.) After the president has made his decision, check and announce his sales for Year I. Ask the company treasurer to fill out a profit and loss statement. Each of the other participants then lists earnings for Year I on Form 1.

(4) Each decision is presented in turn. The order of decisions should not be changed unless same change is made in Form 3. Each new decision involves a yearly profit and loss statement, and individual earnings records. The profit and loss statements must in every case reflect the decisions from previous years, so they should all be kept.

Extensions and variations. One variation, for large classes or for more student participation, is to have two to four companies, with identical instructions to each company president. They would not compete, except to compare profits. In one class in which this was done there was a Red Wodjet Company, a Yellow Wodjet Company, and a Green Wodjet Company, as well as the Blue Wodjet Company. Forms were dittoed in different colored paper so that each company had its own color, and a large bulletin board chart was used to give participants a comparison of company profits.

This idea could be used for specific industries, with some changes. If a class is studying the industry of a particular community, the simulation could be tailored to fit.

There is value in doing this a second time, with different officers.

Debriefing.

1. Discuss how corporations are run and whether this simulation gave the students a better understanding of corporations.
2. Discuss the decisions made, and ask the class whether better ones could have been made.
3. Discuss stocks and the stock market. There are several good stock market board games that could be introduced (see Chapter 10), or use CLASSROOM STOCK MARKET, this chapter.

Assignments.

1. Draw what you think a wodjet looks like.
2. Draw your factory. Design the floor plan and show your office.
3. Draw a map of the city and show where the Blue Wodjet factory is located.
4. Design a pretty stock certificate for the Blue Wodjet company.
5. Design an advertisement for wodjets.

DECISIONS

The indented material is for teacher's information, to be consulted after the decision has been made.

Decision for Year I. To the advertising manager of the company: Your advertising budget has been fairly low in the past few years, and you must decide whether or not to raise it and take a chance that your sales will grow.

Your last year's advertising budget was $5,000. You may, if you wish, raise it, in steps of $5,000, up to $50,000. Consult with the president before making a decision.

Results of decision: (No change in other items on profit and loss statement, except for net profit.)

Advertising budget   *Actual sales*

10,000 3,100,000
15,000 3,200,000
20,000 3,300,000
25,000 . . . . 3,400,000 (optimum)
30,000 3,430,000
35,000 3,435,000
40,000 3,440,000
45,000 3,441,000
50,000 3,442,000

(Note: If the advertising manager decided to leave the advertising budget the same, then sales will remain the same as last year's.

Decision for Year II. To the workers and foremen of the company: A union organizer has come to your plant, and has told you that if you organize a union (which you have not had), you will be able to get higher wages.

If you decide to organize, choose a union leader from your group, and also decide how much increase in wages to demand. The union organizer suggests a 33 ⅓% increase, from which you can come down to 20% or 10% as a result of bargaining, if you wish. He also says that if the company president does not give you any increase, you may go on a strike.

If wages are increased, the increase to the company in labor costs will be on a percentage of last year's:

Last year's labor costs (Year I) $2,000,000
10% increase in wages 2,200,000
20% increase in wages 2,400,000
33 ⅓ increase in wages   2,660,000
(Other percentages are possible, as a result of a compromise.)

If there is a deadlock, or a strike has been called, arbitration is the next step. The union must choose a negotiator, and the management a negotiator, and together the two agree on a third person (from among the townspeople, or the teacher) as the arbitrator. They present their arguments to the arbitrator, and his decision is final.

Decision for Year III. To the production manager: Production experts tell you that if you increase your budget for new machinery they can guarantee you an improvement in your product (blue wodjets), and an increase in sales, because you will then be ahead of your competitors.

They tell you that you can invest from $25,000 to $200,000 more per year in machinery and upkeep, in steps of $25,000. You must decide whether or not to do this, and how much more to invest. There is an optimum limit, at which you have covered the present market. Consult with the president before making a decision.

Results of decision:

Machinery expense (total)	Add to sales
125,000	+ 200,000
150,000	+ 500,000
175,000	+ 800,000
200,000	+1,000,000 (optimum)
225,000	+1,010,000
250,000	+1,015,000
275,000	+1,020,000
300,000	+1,021,000

Decision for Year IV. To the company president: A government pollution inspector has just inspected your plant. He accuses your factory of polluting the air and water, and says you must spend money for pollution control machinery.

There is an element of chance here. Choose a number between one and six, inclusive, to find out how much you must spend for air and water pollution controls for the next five years (Years IV to VIII).

Element of Chance of Pollution Control Expenses:

Number chosen	Total to spend, next five years
1	$150,000 per year.
2	$320,000 per year.
3	$200,000 per year.
4	$310,000 per year.
5	$250,000 per year.
6	$300,000 per year.

To the company president: You must now decide whether to pay the full amount, or take the matter to court. If you decide to pay the full amount, add the costs to the profit and loss statement for this year (and following). If you decide to take the matter to court, court costs to your company will be $10,000 if you lose the case, in addition to other costs. There is an element of chance involved again. Choose a number between one and six, inclusive, to find out the court decision.

Element of Chance in Court Decision

Number chosen   *Court decision*

1 . . . . Government is ordered to give the company credit on income taxes for 10% of the amount spent each year, and to pay all court costs. (You have no court costs, and may deduct 10% of the cost of machinery from taxes.)

2 . . . . Government is ordered to pay 10% of pollution costs each year, and all court costs. (Deduct 10%.)

3 . . . . Government is ordered to pay 25% of pollution costs each year, and all court costs. (Deduct 25%.)

4 . . . . Government is ordered to let the company have ten years to pay the pollution costs. Amount is reduced in half, but extended over the rest of the simulation. Company must pay own court costs.

5 . . . . Company is ordered to pay the full costs over the next five years, or be shut down. Company must also pay court costs.

6 . . . . Government is ordered to give the company credit on income taxes for half of the amount spent each year. Company pays court costs. (Deduct half of the amount from income tax.)

Decision for Year V. To the production manager: A new side line can be developed—polka-dot wodjets. If you invest more money in raw materials, then sales and profits may grow from the new side line. (The present machinery and labor force can produce them with no extra cost.)

You must decide how much to invest, if any. (The side line may or may not make a profit.) You may invest from $20,000 to $100,000 more in raw materials, in units of $20,000. Check with the president before you decide.

Results of decision:

Investment	Increase in sales
$20,000	$25,000
$40,000	$48,000
$60,000	$69,000 (optimum)
$80,000	$70,000
$100,000	$71,000

STOCKHOLDERS MEETINGS:

If, as a result of this year's decision, or any other decision by the company officers, the stockholders become dissatisfied with the profits, they may remove the company president by majority vote at a stockholders meeting. A new president must be selected. The new president may, if he wishes, change the company officers.

Decision for Year VI. To the company president: You have a chance to buy out a competitor, the National Wodjet Company, but you do not have enough money to do so. Your financial experts have suggested a way: sell preferred, non-voting stock, 500 shares at $1000 a share, guaranteed 8% dividends. This would give you enough money. If you decide to buy out the National Wodjet Company, your profits may rise.

If you have decided *yes,* there is an element of chance as to profits. Choose a number between one and six, inclusive.

Results of decision: Amount is profit from the new company, to be added to profit on P & L statement, and deduct the income tax.

Number	Year VI	Year VII	Year VIII	Year IX	Year X
1 . . .	$10,000	$14,000	$20,000	$25,000	$12,500
2 . . .	5,000	10,000	10,000	10,000	5,000
3 . . .	1,000	2,000	4,000	8,000	4,000
4 . . .	50,000	75,000	80,000	85,000	40,000
5 . . .	15,000	20,000	20,000	20,000	10,000
6 . . .	0	25,000	25,000	30,000	15,000

Decision for Year VII. To the sales manager: You have a chance to get a government contract to sell them wodjets of a special design. You must make a bid and see if it is accepted. You may bid at $5.00, $6.00, $7.00, $8.00, $9.00, or $10.00 per wodjet. You must also choose a number between one and six, inclusive. There is a chance your bid may be turned down, if you bid too high.

Results of bid:

Bid	Number chosen (Letters refer to P. & L. items, below.)					
	1	2	3	4	5	6
10.00	H	H	H	H	H	H
9.00	H	A	H	B	A	H
8.00	B	H	C	H	B	A
7.00	C	E	C	D	B	C
6.00	D	E	F	C	D	E
5.00	E	F	G	E	F	G

Increase in Profit & Loss items (add to last year's items):

Letter	Sales	Raw Mat.	Labor	Overh.	Mach.	Gr. Profit
A	1,000,000	100,000	500,000	5,000	10,000	385,000
B	1,000,000	100,000	600,000	10,000	15,000	275,000
C	1,000,000	110,000	700,000	15,000	25,000	150,000
D	500,000	60,000	350,000	5,000	5,000	80,000
E	500,000	65,000	360,000	10,000	10,000	55,000
F	500,000	65,000	370,000	15,000	15,000	35,000
G	400,000	60,000	300,000	10,000	15,000	15,000
H	Bid was turned down by the government.					

Decision for Year VIII. To the sales manager: You have a chance for an overseas contract for your products. You may choose one of the following nations as a customer, and then choose a number between one and six, inclusive: Australia, Brazil, Canada, France, Great Britain, India, Japan, West Germany. (Due to present government restrictions, you cannot choose more than one nation.)

Results of choice and chance. (Letters refer to P & L items, below.)

Nation	Number chosen					
	1	2	3	4	5	6
Australia	F	F	G	G	F	G
Brazil	G	F	F	F	G	F
Canada	F	F	D	E	F	E
France	C	B	B	C	C	D
G. Brit.	B	A	B	A	C	B
India	E	F	G	G	E	F
Japan	A	B	B	A	C	B
W. Germ.	B	B	A	C	A	B

Increase in Profit and Loss items due to above (add to present items):

Letter	Sales	Raw Mat.	Labor	Overhead	Mach.	Gross Profit
A	1,000,000	100,000	500,000	20,000	20,000	360,000
B	1,000,000	100,000	500,000	50,000	50,000	300,000
C	800,000	80,000	400,000	20,000	10,000	290,000
D	800,000	100,000	420,000	30,000	20,000	230,000
E	500,000	65,000	260,000	15,000	15,000	145,000
F	500,000	65,000	280,000	20,000	10,000	125,000
G	400,000	60,000	250,000	10,000	10,000	70,000

Decision for Year IX. To the union leader of the workers: Your company has been getting some new contracts lately, and more profits, and the workers have not had a raise for several years. Now is the year to ask for a wage increase. You may negotiate with the company president. First call a meeting of the workers to decide how much to ask.

Results will depend upon the outcome of the negotiations. Use procedure as outlined in Year II for deadlock or strike.

Decision for Year X. To the company president: A recession has hit the nation. Your sales have been cut in half from last year. (Profits from government contracts and overseas contract, if any, remain the same.)

You must cut your costs to avoid a net loss for the year. You cannot cut the raw materials, overhead, or machinery budget. You might be able to cut the advertising or the labor budget. You could: (1) fire half the workers, and thus cut the labor budget in half; (2) keep the workers, at a lower salary; (3) keep the workers at their present salary, and hope next year will be better; (4) cut your advertising budget.

Results are variable, depending upon the president's action, and reaction of the workers union. A cut in the advertising budget this year would not affect sales.

Profit and Loss Statement for Last Year

Total sales $3,000,000

Expenses:
Cost of raw materials...................$ 500,000.
Labor (and management salaries) .... 2,000,000.
Overhead (heat, lights, taxes) .... 45,000.
Machinery repairs & payments .... 100,000.
Advertising .... 5,000.

Total expenses 2,650,000

Gross profit .... $ 350,000

Less U.S. corporate income taxes .... 122,500.

Net profit for stockholders .... 227,500.
(One thousand shares: $227.50 per share)

The Blue Wodjet Company

Personal Earnings

Name_____   Position_____

My earnings last year .... $_____
My earnings for year I .... $_____
My earnings for year II .... $_____
My earnings for year III .... $_____
My earnings for year IV .... $_____
My earnings for year V .... $_____
My earnings for year VI .... $_____
My earnings for year VII...................... $_____
My earnings for year VIII .... $_____
My earnings for year IX .... $_____
My earnings for year X .... $_____

FORM 1: The Blue Wodjet Company.
(May be dittoed.)

Profit and Loss Statement for the Year _____

Total sales ....$ _____

Cost of raw materials .... $_____

Labor costs & man. salaries .. $_____

Overhead (heat, lights, taxes) . $_____

Machinery repairs & payments $_____

Advertising .... $_____

            Total expenses ......$_____ − _____

            Gross profit ....$_____

            Add gross profits from other

            sources (subsidiaries) .... + _____

            Total profit for the corporation ......$_____

            Less U.S. income tax for corporation − _____

                    (see below)

Net profit to be divided by stockholders ....$_____

(One thousand shares $_____ per share)

U.S. income taxes for corporations in the 1980's:

If gross profit is $1 to $100,000, taxes are 10%.

If gross profit is $100,001 to $200,000, taxes are 20%.

If gross profit is $200,001 to $300,000, taxes are 25%.

If gross profit is $300,001 to $400,000, taxes are 30%.

If gross profit is $400,001 to $500,000, taxes are 35%.

If gross profit is $500,001 to $600,000, taxes are 40%.

If gross profit is $600,001 to $700,000, taxes are 45%.

If gross profit is $700,001 and over, taxes are 50%.

FORM 2: The Blue Wodjet Company.
(May be dittoed.)

EARNINGS SCHEDULE

Code	Last Year	Yr. I	Yr. II	Yr. II	Yr. II	Yr. III	Yr. IV
			(10%)	(20%)	(1/3)		
1.	9,000	9,000	9,900	10,800	12,000	Same as Year II	
2.	10,000	10,000	11,000	12,000	13,200	Same as Year II	
3.	11,000	11,000	12,100	13,200	14,600	Same as Year II	
4.	12,000	12,000	13,200	14,400	16,000	Same as Year II	
5.	13,000	14,000	14,000	14,000	14,000	18,000	18,000
6.	14,000	16,000	16,000	16,000	16,000	20,000	20,000
7.	15,000	15,000	15,000	15,000	15,000	15,000	15,000
8.	16,000	16,000	16,000	16,000	16,000	18,000	18,000
9.	18,000	19,000	19,000	20,000	22,000	22,000	22,000
10.	20,000	20,000	22,000	24,000	26,000	26,000	26,000
11.	22,000	22,000	24,000	26,000	30,000	31,000	31,000
12.	25,000	25,000	25,000	25,000	25,000	25,000	25,000

Code	Year V	Yr. VI	Yr. VII	Yr. VIII	Yr. IX	Yr. X	Strike
1, 2,	Same as in Year II --				Variable	Var.	5,000
3, 4							from union
5.	20,000	20,000	20,000	20,000	20,000	20,000	none
6.	20,000	20,000	20,000	20,000	20,000	20,000	none
7.	16,000	16,000	16,000	16,000	16,000	16,000	16,000
8.	20,000	20,000	20,000	20,000	20,000	20,000	20,000
9.	22,000	23,000	24,000	25,000	27,000	9,000	9,000
10.	26,000	27,000	30,000	32,000	34,000	10,000	10,000
11.	31,000	33,000	35,000	38,000	42,000	none	1,000
12.	25,000	25,000	25,000	25,000	25,000	25,000	25,000

Advertising manager - 5   Production manager - 5
Auto sales company owner - 11   Real estate company owner – 11
Banker - 10   Sales manager - 6
Department store owner - 10   Treasurer - 8
Foreman - 4   Vice-president - 8
Mayor - 7   Workers - 1, 2, or 3.
Newspaper owner - 9
Personnel manager - 5
President of company - 12

FORM 3: The Blue Wodjet Company.
(May be dittoed.)

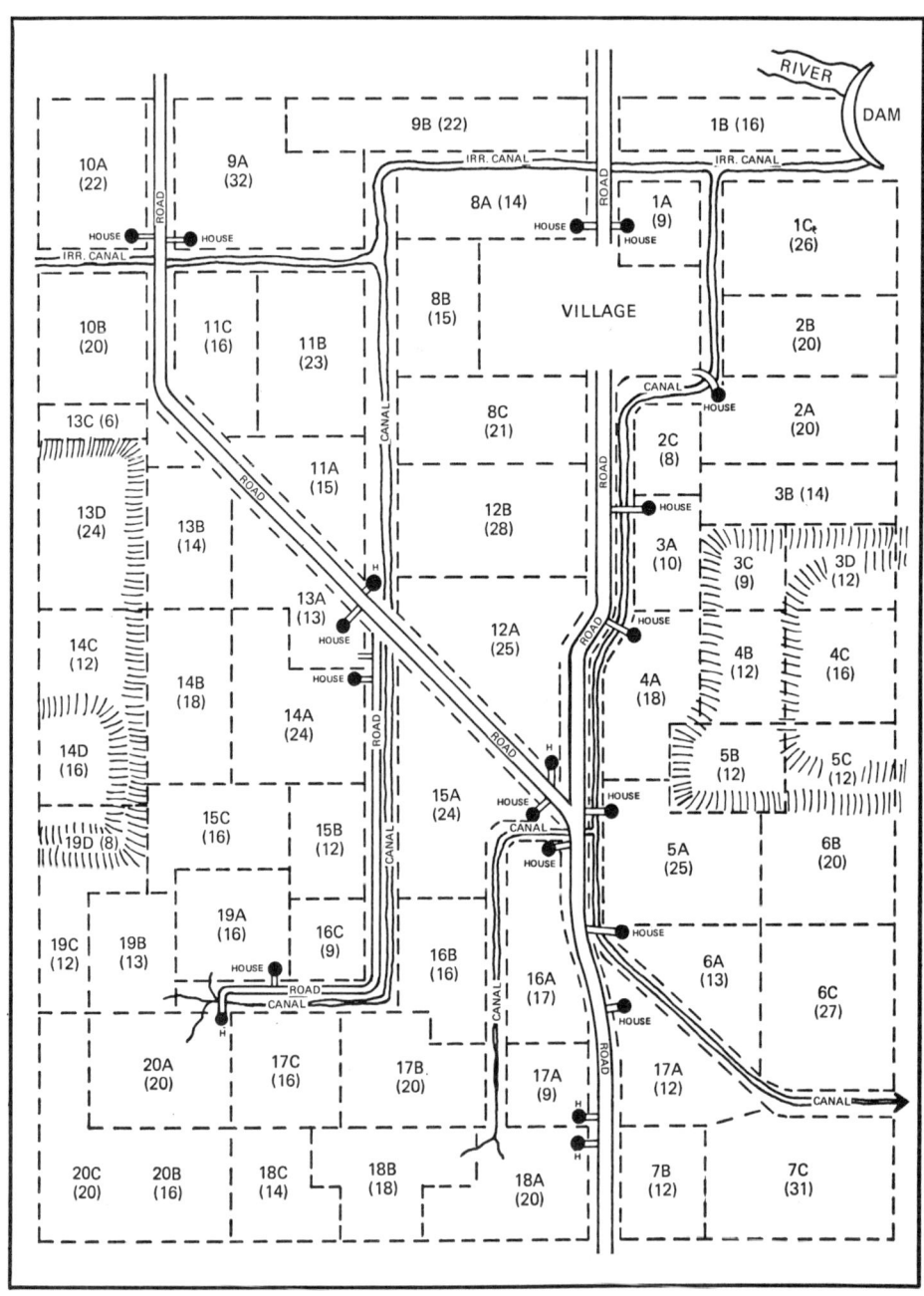

FIGURE 4-1: Map of Farms

LANDOSA

A simulation © 1975 by Jay Reese

Resume. In Landosa the students (as farm owners in an imaginary nation) make decisions about crops to plant, and earn profits. To the students, this is the primary aim of the simulation at first. Gradually they experience a runaway inflation and are forced to deal with it.

Level. Fifth through ninth grades.

Participation. Whole class, singly or in groups (total 20 groups).

Teaching objectives. (1) To enable students to experience a drastic inflation. (2) To enable students to make individual and group decisions. (3) To enable students to verbalize possible causes of inflation and possible cures.

Materials and background needed. *Materials:*

Form A—Farms and Fields (for teacher's use)
Form B— Background Information on Landosa (for students' use)
Form C—List of Costs and Returns (for teacher's use)
Form D—List of Returns (for teacher's use)
Form E—Farm Report (for students' use)
Form F—Representative Prices in Landosa
Form G—Government Bond (for students' use)
Xeroxed maps of farms. (See Figure 4-1.)

Background: None necessary for average classes.

Getting ready. (1) Let the class form into twenty groups, corresponding to the number of farms. (There could be less than twenty.) Since persons in reality have no choice into which family they are born, assigning of the farms should be done by lot.

(2) Choose a banker to keep accounts.

(3) Each farm group will start with "inherited" money in the bank. To determine how much, ask each group to choose a letter between A and H, inclusive, and a number between 1 and 6, inclusive. Example, A6. Consult the chart below:

	1	2	3	4	5	6
A	none	5,000	100	400	1,000	1,000
B	500	200	none	800	5,000	400
C	100	300	1,000	8,000	200	2,000
D	1,000	none	300	100	300	300

	1	2	3	4	5	6
E	400	100	500	none	500	500
F	800	400	5,000	500	100	8,000
G	3,000	800	200	1,000	none	800
H	200	3,000	4,000	5,000	1,500	200

The amount given is the "inheritance" with which each begins the game.

To play. (a) Reading from Form A, or from the map, tell each landowner how many hectares he/she has, and what type. There are four types of land: irrigated valley land, non-irrigated valley land, low upland, and high upland.

(2) Read or give each student a copy of the background information (Form B). Each landowner must decide what to plant on his land. His choice is limited:

Irrigated valley land: wheat, alfalfa, vineyards, or fruit.
Non-irrigated valley land: grazing, wheat or vineyards.
Low upland: grazing, wheat, or vineyards.
High upland: grazing only.

Each crop requires an initial investment, except grazing. (One Landosa lann equals one U.S. dollar, to start.) Apples, peaches, pears are 5 lanns per hectares; alfalfa, 1 lann per hectare; vineyards, 10 lanns per hectare; irrigated wheat, 2 lanns per hectare; non-irrigated wheat, 1 lann per hectare. This initial investment is to be taken from the landowner's bank account. If he has no money, he must apply for a loan, which will be granted by the bank automatically, to be repaid by the end of the sixth year with ten percent interest per year.

(3) After all farmers have given their decisions, teacher consults Forms C and D and announces results (the amount of net profit gained that year, per hectare): grazing, 10 lanns; non-irrigated wheat, 13 lanns; irrigated wheat, 25 lanns; alfalfa, 15 lanns. Apples pay 2 lanns; peaches, pears, pay 2 lanns; vineyards, pay 5 lanns. Those students who are receiving money may fill out Form E and give it to the banker. Others must have the amount they pay deducted from their bank accounts.

(4) *Second year.* Before starting this year, announce to the class, "President Marcola of Landosa has begun an ambitious building program in the capital. He is building a new capitol building, a new presidential palace, and a new national theater. He has had to borrow money to pay for this, making the national debt higher. One lann is now worth seventy-five U.S. cents. (One and one-third lanns will buy one U.S. dollar.)"

Students go through the same procedure of deciding what to plant (though those with vineyards and fruit should not change their crops), and then teacher should consult Forms C and D and announce the results. (Note that costs to plant new crops are higher this year.) Students again fill out Form E.

(Lanns may be exchanged for U.S. dollars at the exchange rate whenever students wish to do so, or vice versa.)

(5) *Third year.* Before starting, announce, "President Marcola's building program is continuing. He has also given all government workers, including the military, a generous raise in pay. Welfare costs have also risen. He has had to borrow more money and raise the national debt to run the government this year. One lann is now worth 50¢ U.S. (Two lanns will buy one U.S. dollar.)"

The yearly procedure is conducted.

(6) *Fourth year.* Announce, "One lann is now worth 30¢ U.S. (Three and one-third lanns will buy one U.S. dollar.) This is election year. President Marcola, who promises to control the inflation, is running again. He is also promising to raise all government salaries and welfare costs and pay for them by a 'new secret plan.' His opponent is Mr. Wendly, who says *he* will control the inflation and that Marcola will only make it worse. At the end of the year, you will know who won."

Go through the yearly procedure, and then announce, "Marcola was re-elected President of Landosa for another four-year term. He will announce his plans to control the inflation at the beginning of next year."

(7) *Fifth year.* Announce, "One lann is now worth 20¢ U.S. (Five lanns will buy one U.S. dollar.) President Marcola has announced his new plan to control inflation: Everyone will have to buy Landosa government bonds, which the government will pay off in ten years (but not before that time), and will also pay interest. Everyone who earns more than ten thousand lanns a year will have to pay half his income above ten thousand lanns into these government bonds. In other words, if a person earns twenty thousand lanns, he will have to buy five thousand lanns of government bonds."

Go through the routine for this year, and then each student at the end of the year must put half of his year's earnings (above ten thousand lanns) into government bonds. Use Form G.

(8) *7th through 10th years.* Consult Forms C and E and announce the changes in the currency and inflation each year. The 8th year is another election year, and President Marcola is running for another term. His re-election could be made a matter of chance, if you wish—

rolling a die and taking an even number as his re-election, and an odd number his defeat. The yearly routine is done each year.

You may end the simulation at any year, or use one of the variations listed below, particularly variation 4, the Landosa Senate.

Discussion. As a debriefing exercise, the class could benefit by a discussion of the inflation and what the weakening of the currency meant to them. The lucky few (if any) who put their money into U.S. dollars near the beginning of the inflation might wish to comment on how they felt. This might stimulate a discussion as to the possible causes of Landosa's inflation (overspending by the government; printing more money), and possible cures.

Who gets hurt the most by inflation? Who gets hurt the least?

Variations and complications.

1. Some classes need to have the inflationary period accelerated for better effect. You may use years 1, 3, 5, 7, and 9 and skip the others.

2. Allow students an option to buy gold at the current world market price, adjusted for the degree of inflation in Landosa.

3. To make the inflation more realistic, post prices for some representative products and change these prices as the inflation grows worse. Form F is such a suggested list.

4. During Year 7 or later, turn the class into the Landosa Senate Pretend President Marcola has been overthrown, or resigned, and now they, the Senate, must find a way to end the inflation. Currency devaluation might be one means.

Assignments.

1. Do research on ruinous inflation in foreign countries such as Germany in the early 1920's, and Hungary in 1945-46. What caused the inflation? How did it affect the people? What ended the inflation?

2. Play the game *Beat Inflation* by Avalon Hill (see Chapter 10) and report on how you could protect yourself against inflation.

3. Collect stamps and show how inflation has changed the cost of mailing a letter in the United States and elsewhere.

4. Look in a few recent World Almanacs and report on the inflation trends in the U.S. and foreign nations during the past few years.

Farm 1—51 hectares. Field 1A, 9 irrigated valley hectares. Field 1B, 16 irrigated valley hectares. Field 1C, 26 irrigated valley hectares.

Farm 2—48 hectares. Field 2A, 20 irrigated valley hectares. Field 2B, 20 irrigated valley hectares. Field 2C, 8 irrigated valley hectares.

Farm 3—55 hectares. Field 3A, 10 irrigated valley hectares. Field 3B, 14 non-irrigated valley hectares. Field 3C, 19 low upland hectares. Field 3D, 12 high upland hectares.

Farm 4—46 hectares. Field 4A, 18 irrigated valley hectares. Field 4B, 12 low upland hectares. Field 4C, 16 high upland hectares.

Farm 5—49 hectares. Field 5A, 25 irrigated valley hectares. Field 5B, 12 low upland hectares. Field 5C, 12 high upland hectares.

Farm 6—60 hectares. Field 6A, 13 irrigated valley hectares. Field 6B, 20 non-irrigated valley hectares. Field 6C, 27 irrigated valley hectares.

Farm 7—55 hectares. Field 7A, 12 irrigated valley hectares. Field 7B, 12 non-irrigated valley hectares. Field 7C, 31 irrigated valley hectares.

Farm 8—50 hectares. Field 8A, 14 irrigated valley hectares. Field 8B, 15 irrigated valley hectares. Field 8C, 21 irrigated valley hectares.

Farm 9—54 hectares. Field 9A, 32 irrigated valley hectares. Field 9B, 22 irrigated valley hectares.

Farm 10—42 hectares. Field 10A, 22 irrigated valley hectares. Field 10B, 20 irrigated valley hectares.

Farm 11—54 hectares. Field 11A, 15 irrigated valley hectares. Field 11B, 23 irrigated valley hectares. Field 11C, 16 irrigated valley hectares.

Farm 12—53 hectares. Field 12A, 25 irrigated valley hectares. Field 12B, 28 irrigated valley hectares.

Farm 13—52 hectares. Field 13A, 13 irrigated valley hectares. Field 13B, 14 non-irrigated valley hectares. Field 13C, 6 non-irrigated valley hectares. Field 13D, 24 low upland hectares.

Farm 14—70 hectares. Field 14A, 24 irrigated valley hectares. Field 14B, 18 non-irrigated valley hectares. Field 14C, 12 low upland hectares. Field 14D, 16 high upland hectares.

Farm 15—52 hectares. Field 15A, 24 irrigated valley hectares. Field 15B, 12 irrigated valley hectares. Field 15C, 16 non-irrigated valley hectares.

Farm 16—42 hectares. Field 16A, 17 irrigated valley hectres. Field 16B, 16 irrigated valley hectares. Field 16C, 9 irrigated valley hectares.

Farm 17—45 hectares. Field 17A, 9 irrigated valley hectares. Field 17B, 20 irrigated valley hectares. Field 17C, 16 irrigated valley hectares.

Farm 18—52 hectares. Field 18A, 20 irrigated valley hectares. Field 18B, 18 irrigated valley hectares. Field 18C, 14 non-irrigated valley hectares.

Farm 19—49 hectares. Field 19A, 16 irrigated valley hectares. Field 19B, 13 irrigated valley hectares. Field 19C, 12 non-irrigated valley hectares. Field 19D, 8 high upland hectares.

Farm 20—56 hectares. Field 20A, 20 irrigated valley hectares. Field 20B, 16 non-irrigated valley hectares. Field 20C, 20 non-irrigated valley hectares.

FORM A: Landosa. (For teachers.) FARMS AND FIELDS

Landosa is a small nation located somewhere on the planet Earth. It is primarily an agricultural nation.

Landosa's money unit is called a "lann." One lann is equal to one United States dollar on exchange, at the present time.

You are the owner or co-owner of one of the large farms located in the Main Valley of Landosa. You belong to the upper class of the nation. You employ lower-class workers at fair wages.

You will begin this simulation by finding out how much money you have inherited as you take over this farm. Give the teacher a number between 1 and 6, and a letter between A and H (example, 6H). You will then be notified as to how much money (if any) you will have to begin.

Your next job is to decide what to grow on your farm. Your choice is limited.

On *irrigated valley land,* you may grow wheat, alfalfa, peaches, pears, apples, or vineyards. Or you may use it for grazing. You will have to pay for seed or seedlings (and water if you irrigated). Costs are: apples, 5 lanns per hectares; alfalfa, one lann per hectare; irrigated wheat, 2 lanns per hectare; peaches or pears, 5 lanns per hectare; vineyards, 10 lanns per hectare. (Grazing is no cost.) Remember, if you plant fruit trees or vineyards, it will take a few years before you make a profit on them, but once you do your profit will probably be much greater than from other crops.

On *non-irrigated valley land,* you may grow wheat or vineyards. Non-irrigated wheat costs 1 lann per hectare; vineyards cost 10 lanns per hectare. Or you may use the land for grazing at no cost.

On low upland, you may grow wheat or vineyards, or use the land for grazing. Costs are the same as for non-irrigated valley land.

On *high upland,* you may only have grazing.

You may change your mind each year as to what to grow in each field. But some crops such as fruit and vineyards take a few years to reach full production. Also, if you have fruit trees growing and want to plant wheat instead, you will have to pay an extra three lanns per hectare to have the trees removed. For vineyards it costs two lanns to have them removed. This is in addition to your regular planting costs.

You also have a choice as to what to do with your profits. The teacher will tell you at the end of each year what your profits are (after paying all expenses, living costs, and taxes). You may either: (1) keep it in a local Landosan bank; (3) take it in cash (and take a chance it will be lost or stolen); or (3) convert it into U.S. dollars and put it in a U.S. bank. (Though one lann is now worth one U.S. dollar, the value may change each year.) (4) You may also invest it in five-year Landosan Government bonds which pay interest. You may buy a 100-lann bond for 75 lanns, a 500-lann bond for 375 lanns, and a 1000-lann bond for 750 lanns.

FORM B: Landosa. (For students.) BACKGROUND INFORMATION.
(May be dittoed.)

Year ---------		1	2	3	4	5	6	7	8	9	10
Crop:		Return per hectare (after expenses & taxes):									
Alfalfa	Cons.	15	13	20	5	25	20	25	5	2 1/2	15
	Infl.	15	17	40	17	125	200	500	500	2500	150,000
Apples	Cons.	pay 2	pay 5	0	25	50	75	100	100	0	100
	Infl.	pay 2	pay 8	0	83	250	750	2500	10,000	0	1,000,000
Grazing	Cons.	10	7	5	13	13	2	13	13	5	10
	Infl.	10	9	10	43	65	20	260	1300	5,000	100,000
Irr. Wheat	Cons.	25	20	25	23	30	25	38	25	38	25
	Infl.	25	26	50	76	150	250	760	2500	38,000	250,000
Non-Irr. Wheat	Cons.	13	10	2	13	25	0	13	25	3	12
	Infl.	13	13	4	43	125	0	260	2500	3,000	120,000
Peaches	Cons.	pay 2	5	0	13	25	30	40	40	20	40
	Infl.	pay 2	6	0	43	125	300	800	4000	20,000	400,000
Pears	Cons.	pay 2	5	0	15	30	50	60	50	10	30
	Infl.	pay 2	6	0	50	150	500	1200	5000	10,000	300,000
Vineyards	Cons.	pay 5	10	15	25	50	60	80	100	80	100
	Infl.	pay 5	12	30	83	250	600	1600	10,000	120,000	1,000,000
Crop		Crop to plant new (for fruit, use Form E for ensuing years)									
Alfalfa, non-irr. wheat.		1	1	2	3	5	10	20	100	100	10,000
Apples, peaches, pears.		5	6	10	16	25	50	100	500	5000	50,000
Irr. Wheat		2	2	4	6	10	20	40	200	2000	20,000
Vineyards		10	13	20	33	50	100	200	1000	10,000	100,000
		Amount of inflation (U.S. dollars)									
1 lann -		$1	75¢	50¢	30¢	20¢	10¢	5¢	1¢	1/10¢	1/100¢
1 U.S. dollar -	Lanns:	1	1 1/3	2	3 1/3	5	10	20	100	1000	10,000

FORM C: Landosa. Teacher's List of Costs and Returns.
Crop schedule for those who plant apples, peaches, pears, or vineyards after first year. Amount given is the "constant" return perhectare in lanns. You must adjust for inflation.

	Year of planting	1st year following	2nd year following	3rd year following	4th year following	5th year following	6th year following
Apples	pay 5	pay 2	pay 5	5	25	50	75
Peaches	pay 5	pay 2	5	5	10	25	30
Pears	pay 5	pay 2	5	5	10	15	20
Vineyards	pay 10	pay 5	10	15	25	50	60

FORM D: Landosa. Teacher's List of Returns.
Crop schedule for those who plant apples, peaches, pears, or vineyards after first year. Amount given is the "constant" return per hectare in lanns. You must adjust for inflation.

Farm:_____   Year:_____

Field   Crop   Hectares× Cost = Total Cost
_____ _____ _____×_____ =_____
_____ _____ _____×_____ =_____
_____ _____ _____×_____ =_____
_____ _____ _____×_____ =_____

                                  Total cost _____

To Banker:
    1. Withdraw_____lanns from my/our account.
    2. Deposit_____lanns to my/our account.
    3. Pay me/us_____lanns in cash.
    4. Change_____lanns to U.S. dollars and deposit in the
       American Bank.

Banker: Checked for accuracy_____   Money transaction completed_____

FORM E: Landosa. (For students.) FARM REPORT.
(May be dittoed.)

	Yr. 1	Year 2	Yr. 3	Yr. 4	Yr. 5	Yr. 6	Yr. 7	Yr. 8	Yr. 9	Yr. 10
Imported goods:										
Airplane (used)	5000	6600	10,000	16,600	25,000	50,000	100,000	500,000	5,000,000	50,000,000
Auto (used)	4000	5300	8,000	13,300	20,000	40,000	80,000	400,000	4,000,000	40,000,000
Color TV	500	660	1,000	1660	2500	5000	10,000	50,000	500,000	5,000,000
B & W TV	200	260	400	660	1000	2000	4000	20,000	200,000	2,000,000
Pr. Shoes	25	33	50	83	125	250	500	2500	25,000	250,000
Trans. Radio	5	7	10	17	25	50	100	500	5000	50,000
Gasoline (liter)	.20	.26	.40	.66	1	2	4	20	200	2000
Locally-made goods; and products:										
Pr. Shoes	5	7	10	17	25	50	100	500	5000	50,000
Btle of pop	.10	.13	.20	.30	.50	1	2	10	100	1000
Candy bar	.05	.07	.10	.15	.25	.50	1	5	50	500
Dz. eggs	.50	.66	1	1.50	2.50	5	10	50	500	5000
Mlk cow	40	50	80	120	200	400	800	4000	40,000	400,000
Beef cow	20	25	40	60	100	200	400	2000	20,000	200,000
Horse	50	65	100	150	250	500	1000	5000	50,000	500,000
Local service:										
Haircut	.30	.40	.60	.90	1.25	3	6	30	300	3000
Postage stamp	.10	.13	.20	.30	.50	1	2	10	100	1000
Av. wage (hour)	1	1.30	2	3.30	5	10	20	100	100	10,000

FORM F: REPRESENTATIVE PRICES IN LANDOSA. (See extension.)

• •

REPUBLIC OF LANDOSA - - BOND
FIVE YEARS after date of issue given below, THE GOVERN-
MENT OF THE REPUBLIC OF LANDOSA will pay to
_____
or his/her assigns, the sum of_____
Lanns (L _____ . ____).
          THIS BOND IS NOT REDEEMABLE BEFORE THE DUE DATE. It
may be redeemed at any time after five years of date of issuance.
          Issued _____ , 19 ____.

                              Y.A. Arbelos
                              Minister of Treasury
                              REPUBLIC OF LANDOSA

• •
• •

          Costs:
                    100 - Lann bond : 75 Lanns
                    500 - Lann bond : 750 Lanns
                   1000 - Lann bond : 750 Lanns
                   5000 - Lann bond : 3750 Lanns
                 10,000 - Lann bond : 7500 Lanns
                 50,000 - Lann bond : 37,500 Lanns
                100,000 - Lann bond : 75,000 Lanns
                500,000 - Lann bond : 375,000 Lanns
              1,000,000 - Lann bond : 750,000 Lanns

• •

FORM G: Landosa. GOVERNMENT BOND.
(May be dittoed.)

GALACTICA

Resume. Students are traders from various planets with specialized goods to trade and specific goods to obtain, in a limited time. They have money but it is worthless in figuring final points.

Grade levels. Best for grades five through seven.

Time. Played in rounds of five minutes each. One game may take several rounds.

Participation. Twenty or more students.

Teaching objectives. (1) To experience the give and take of a barter system. (2) To experience use of a money system in which the value is nil. (3) To design strategies of trading in order to meet specific objectives.

Materials needed. (1) Trading cards (12 of each needed). See Figure 4-2.
(2) Money (60 units needed). See Figure 4-3.
(3) Directions for each planet (one or two copies for each group needed). See Figure 4-4.
(4) Numbers for desks or tables (one through ten, one each).

Getting ready. Divide the class into ten groups. An optimum is two students per group, though there can be more or less. There cannot be less than ten students, however, because each group (planet) needs to be represented.

Give the students the following background information, orally or dittoed:

> You are all traders from various planets in the Milky Way Galaxy. Each group represents a different planet. Your planet has one type of goods to trade, and has various types of goods you want.
>
> You may choose a name for your planet if you wish.
>
> Because transportation by space ship is so expensive, only very expensive or unusual items are worth trading. Since each planet has one item no other planet has, you may use these to trade. You will each also begin with six units of currency called Galactic Trade Dollars (GT$), and you may use these in trading.
>
> Each planet has only one space ship (for a trader to use in going to other planets). One player from each group may visit the other groups with goods to trade. The other player(s) from that group must stay at their home table and barter with the traders who visit them.
>
> Rules of trade: Anything may be traded for anything, in any amount. This includes GT$.

ONE CARGO LOAD OF

ZIGGAS

from Planet One. Ziggas are small animals that make outstanding pets.

ONE CARGO LOAD OF

YERGIS

from Planet Two. Yergis are plants that make cosmetics that will make all women appear sixteen years old.

ONE CARGO LOAD OF

XALPAS

from Planet Three. Xalpas are plants that make spices that are an entirely new taste sensation.

ONE CARGO LOAD OF

WILTINIAS

from Planet Four. Wiltinias are gems that resemble diamonds but sparkle with all colors of the rainbow.

ONE CARGO LOAD OF

VOLPAS

from Planet Five. Volpas are plants that make medicines that will cure the common cold.

ONE CARGO LOAD OF

URGA NUTS

from Planet Six. Urga Nuts taste like bananas, ice cream, marshmallows, and chocolate.

ONE CARGO LOAD OF

TOOLIES

from Planet Seven. Toolies are fruits that make every other fruit taste like paste in comparison.

ONE CARGO LOAD OF

SI LEAVES

from Planet Eight. Si Leaves make a beverage that is tasteful, filling, non-narcotic, and non-fattening.

ONE CARGO LOAD OF

ROBOTS

from Planet Nine. Robots are metal servants that will do any and all household and office tasks, and also entertain.

ONE CARGO LOAD OF

QUINZZES

from Planet Ten. Quinzzes are berries that taste delicious, have no calories, have all the needed vitamins and minerals, and help in reducing weight.

FIGURE 4-2: Trading Cards. (12 of each needed; duplicate on heavy paper or cardboard.)

ONE   ONE   ONE   ONE   ONE   ONE   ONE   ONE   ONE   ONE   ONE

THIS IS ONE GALACTIC TRADE DOLLAR

It is valid for whatever value is placed upon it.

Certified genuine:

R. U. Shoor

Treasurer

1   1   1   1   1   1   1   1   1   1   1   1

ONE   ONE   ONE   ONE   ONE   ONE   ONE   ONE   ONE   ONE   ONE

THIS IS ONE GALACTIC TRADE DOLLAR

It is valid for whatever value is placed upon it.

Certified genuine:

R. U. Shoor

Treasurer

1   1   1   1   1   1   1   1   1   1   1   1

ONE   ONE   ONE   ONE   ONE   ONE   ONE   ONE   ONE   ONE   ONE

THIS IS ONE GALACTIC TRADE DOLLAR

It is valid for whatever value is placed upon it.

Certified genuine:

R. U. Shoor

Treasurer

1   1   1   1   1   1   1   1   1   1   1   1

FIGURE 4-3: Galactica Money

Planet One. You have twelve ZIGGAS to trade. Ziggas are animals that make excellent pets.

You need one Robot from Planet Nine, one Quinzz from Planet Ten, one Volpa from Planet Five, two Xalpas from Planet Three, four Yergis from Planet Two, and three Si Leaves from Planet Eight.

Planet Two. You have twelve YERGIS to trade. Yergis are cosmetic plants.

You need two Robots from Planet Nine, one Quinzz from Planet Ten, one Volpa from Planet Five, one Xalpa from Planet Three, three Ziggas from Planet One, and four Si Leaves from Planet Eight.

Planet Three. You have twelve XALPAS (zalpas) to trade. Xalpas are plants that make spices.

You need three Robots from Planet Nine, one Quinzz from Planet Ten, two Volpas from Planet Five, one Si Leaf from Planet Eight, one Zigga from Planet One, and four Yergis from Planet Two.

Planet Four. You have twelve WILTINIAS to trade. Wiltinias are gems.

You need three Quinzzes from Planet Ten, two Volpas from Planet Five, one Xalpa from Planet Three, three Urga Nuts from Planet Six, one Yergi from Planet Two, and two Toolies from Planet Seven.

Planet Five. You have twelve VOLPAS to trade. Volpas are medicinal plants.

You need three Robots from Planet Nine, four Toolies from Planet Seven, one Xalpa from Planet Three, two Wiltinias from Planet Four, one Urga Nut from Planet Six, and one Xalpa from Planet Three.

Planet Six. You have twelve URGA NUTS for trade.

You need two Quinzzes from Planet Ten, four Si Leaves from Planet Eight, one Volpa from Planet Five, two Wiltinias from Planet Four, one Xalpa from Planet Three, and two Ziggas from Planet One.

Planet Seven. You have twelve TOOLIES to trade. Toolies are fruit.

You need one Robot from Planet Nine, four Urga Nuts from Planet Six, one Volpa from Planet Five, two Wiltinias from Planet Four, two Xalpas from Planet Three, and two Yergis from Planet Two.

FIGURE 4-4: Directions for Each Planet

Planet Eight. You have twelve SI LEAVES for trade. Si Leaves make beverages.

You need one Robot from Planet Nine, one Quinzz from Planet Ten, one Volpa from Planet Five, two Wiltinias from Planet Four, one Xalpa from Planet Three, and six Ziggas from Planet One.

Planet Nine. You have twelve ROBOTS for trade. Robots are metal servants.

You need three Quinzzes from Planet Ten, two Urga Nuts from Planet Six, two Volpas from Planet Five, two Wiltinias from Planet Four, two Xalpas from Planet Three, and one Toolie from Planet Seven.

Planet Ten. You have twelve QUINZZES for trade. Quinzzes are berries.

You need one Robot from Planet Nine, five Toolies from Planet Seven, one Volpa from Planet Five, two Wiltinias from Planet Four, one Xalpa from Planet Three, and two Urga Nuts from Planet Six.

FIGURE 4-4 (continued)

Planet	Goods for Sale	Q	R	S	T	U	V	W	X	Y	Z
One	Ziggas	1*1		3	0	0	1	0	2	4	-
Two	Yergis	1	2	4	0	0	1	0	1	-	3
Three	Xalpas	1	3	1	0	0	2	0	-	4	1
Four	Wiltinias	3	0	0	2	3	2	-	1	1	0
Five	Volpas	0	3	0	4	1	-	2	1	1	0
Six	Urga Nuts	2	0	4	0	-	1	2	1	0	2
Seven	Toolies	0	1	0	-	4	1	2	2	2	0
Eight	Si Leaves	1	1	-	0	0	1	2	1	0	6
Nine	Robots	3	-	0	1	2	2	2	0	0	0
Ten	Quinzzes	-	1	0	5	2	1	2	1	0	0

*Numerals represent the amount of each type of goods needed. For instance, a "1" under the Q means "one Quinzz card needed."

FIGURE 4-5: List of Planets and Goods Wanted. (Teacher copy.)

Each planet has a list of objectives and where to get them, but does not know the objectives of the other planets. It is best to keep your own objectives a secret. (See Figure 4-5.)

At the end, you will get a point for each of the goods you get that is on your list, and the group or groups with the largest number of points wins. (No point will be given for any money you have on hand at the end.)

Next distribute the twelve trade cards for each planet, the six units of currency, and the list of goods wanted. Each group should have a number to correspond with the number of their planet, and this should be fastened on their desk or table, so others will know what planet they represent.

The length of each trading session is five minutes. Ask all traders to return to their home planet at the end of that time. If there is no winner, i.e., no one who has completed a list, allow another five minutes. Play goes for the entire five minutes, even though one or more groups may have achieved their objectives. At the end, when at least one group has finished, count the scores. The group or groups with the highest score wins (twelve points is a maximum). No points will be given for GT$, or for more goods above the limit of their objectives.

Debriefing. Discuss such questions as:

1. How many planet groups obtained their objectives?
2. How did trading strategies develop?
3. How did traders advertise?
4. How many planetary groups had extra GT$'s (more than six) at the end?
5. How many traders realized GT$'s were worthless? (Or were they?)
6. Did many GT$'s change hands during the trading sessions?
7. What makes the value of money?
8. Was there a need for a central market place, or a central buyer? Would it have helped the game?

Extensions and variations.

1. It would seem profitable to try the simulation a second time, and this time give the GT$ a value—that is, give a point at the end for each GT$ held. A good comparison of the results could be made at the debriefing.

2. One or two more planets could be added, with no goods for

trade, but just with GT$. (They would have to have their own lists of items to buy.)

3. A central buyer could be appointed, given GT$, and empowered to buy items and resell them.

Assignments.

1. Do research on money and currency, and report on what it means to have a "barter system" compared to having currency.

2. What makes the value of metal coins? What are they really worth? Does a penny have a cent's worth of copper in it? Does a nickel have five cents' worth of metal? Do research on it and report.

3. Do research on the phrase "legal tender" and what it means.

4. Do research on the different types of currency in foreign nations today, and how much their unit of currency is in U.S. dollars.

CLASSROOM STOCK MARKET

Resume. Students buy stocks in corporations formed to buy *Monopoly* properties, elect officers, and collect dividends. A stock market board lists stocks and current market value.

Grade levels. Recommended for grades five through nine.

Participation. Whole class. Works best to about thirty students.

Teaching objectives. (1) To learn about the operation of a stock market. (2) To learn how corporations are run. (3) To experience buying and selling of stocks.

Materials needed.

1. One complete *Monopoly* game.
2. Extra *Monopoly* money.[1]
3. Blank stock shares.
4. Stockholder lists (at least ten needed).
5. Stock order forms (optional).
6. Balance sheet forms.
7. Copy of a *Monopoly* board for bulletin board.[2]
8. Green houses and red hotels made of construction paper for bulletin board.

---

[1]*Monopoly* money may be purchased at toy and hobby stores. It is best to backstamp the money with an individual stamp so that students will not bring additional money from home.

[2]Unmounted *Monopoly* boards, called "Monopoly Labels," are available from Parker Brothers, P.O. Box 900, Salem, Mass. 01970 for 50¢ each.

Getting ready. (1) Duplicate the forms needed (see Figures 4-6 through 4-11).

(2) Put up the bulletin board.

(3) Give each player $300 in *Monopoly* money.

(4) Choose at least one banker (a non-player).

(5) Choose at least one stockbroker (a non-player).

(6) Post or distribute a list of stocks available to buy.

To play. (1) Players decide which stocks they want to buy and how many, fill out stock order forms, and give them to the stockbroker. (The reason for order forms is so that stockbroker can fill orders during his/her spare time, and hand out stock shares during the next round.) It is best to end at this point and start the next step a day or so later.

(2) After all players have received the stocks they ordered, each corporation has a stockholders meeting in which a president is chosen, and other officers (vice-president, treasurer). These officers hold the corporation's money, buy property, and make decisions. At the stockholders meetings, each stockholder gets votes equal to his shares—if he/she owns twenty shares, this is twenty votes.

(3) Corporation officers then submit written bids for unimproved *Monopoly* properties. There is no form for this—they just write down the name of the property and their bid. Bids must not be below the minimum. In case of a tie bid, flip a coin. Corporation officers receive the property deeds after paying banker for them.

(4) Corporation officers buy houses (and hotels) as they wish. Banker or stockbroker pins the construction paper houses and hotels to the property on the bulletin board sheet. *Monopoly* houses and hotels could be taped on with transparent tape, but this might not prove too feasible. This could end this round.

(5) There are six imaginary players on the *Monopoly* board, with unlimited bank accounts. These now start. Colored map pins can represent the players on the bulletin board. Banker and stockbroker roll dice and play one round (each of the six getting one move) as per regular *Monopoly* game. The players cannot buy property, and when they draw the Community Chest or Chance cards, they ignore all except those that give movement (i.e., "Move to Illinois Avenue"). They can go to Jail but must get out on the next move.

(6) Corporations receive the money as the six imaginary players land on their property.

(7) Each round henceforth is one complete move for all six players.

At a set time during each round, students may buy or sell stocks as they wish. Stocks may be sold or traded between students, but banker must keep a list of current stock owners.

(8) Banker must call for balance sheets periodically, usually at the end of each round. After they are filed, stockbroker uses them and with the formula shown in Figure 4-11 determines the current market value of each stock. He posts that on the board.

(9) Corporation officers may declare dividends if they wish, and distribute the money to their stockholders, or they may keep all of the dividends as assets.

(10) There is no set limit on this simulation. I would suggest about ten rounds. It depends upon the interest of the students. You may wish to use some of the variations suggested on page 108.

CONGLOMERATE, INC. 100 shares at $10.
PROPERTIES, INC. 100 shares at $10.
RENTALS, INC. 100 shares at $10.
FUSCHIA CORPORATION 100 shares at $20.
AQUA CORPORATION 100 shares at $20.
MAUVE CORPORATION 100 shares at $30.
VELVET CORPORATION 100 shares at $40.
ROYAL CORPORATION 100 shares at $40.

FIGURE 4-6: List of Corporations with Shares to Sell, and Prices

---

Any bids under this price will be turned down. Bids may be made as high above as you wish.

THE FOUR RAILROADS $800.
THE TWO UTILITIES $300.
PURPLE GROUP (Mediterranean, Baltic) $100.
LIGHT BLUE GROUP (Oriental, Vermont, Connecticut) $300.
MAROON GROUP (St. Charles, States, Virginia) $400.
ORANGE GROUP (St. James, Tennessee, New York) $550.
RED GROUP (Kentucky, Illinois, Indiana) $650.
YELLOW GROUP (Atlantic, Ventnor, Marvin Gardens) $700.
GREEN GROUP (Pacific, North Carolina, Pennsylvania) $900.
DARK BLUE GROUP (Park Place, Boardwalk) $800.

FIGURE 4-7: Minimum Bids for Properties on the *Monopoly* Board

This certifies that _____ owns _____
shares of stock in the _____ Corporation.
Signed _____
Broker

- -

STOCKHOLDER LIST for _____ Corporation:

Name	Number of shares	Price paid

FIGURE 4-8: Stock Share

Name of Corporation .... Date_____
Total value of Land (Deeds) .... $_____
Total value of Houses .... $_____
Total value of Hotels .... $_____
Cash on hand .... $_____
Other assets .... $_____
Total Assets .... $_____

There are _____ shares of stock issued, so each share of stock is
now worth $_____ (Divide total assets by number of shares.)

Signed:

_____

FIGURE 4-9: Balance Sheet. (To be filled out by Corporation President or Treasurer and turned in.)

I would like to buy the following:

Number of shares	Corporation	Price per share	Total

Total Enclosed $_____

FIGURE 4-10: Stock Order Form. (To be filled out and turned in to stockbroker with money.)

1. If the total assets are enough so that each shareholder could get at least $1 per share (if it were divided evenly), the market value of each share goes to an amount more than the original. For instance, if the Mauve Corporation had enough assets so that each shareholder would get $33 (instead of $30 that was paid), the market value of Mauve is $33.

2. If there are corporations in which no one bought stock, lower the market value per share by one-fifth or one-fourth. For instance, if after the first round no one bought shares in the Velvet Corporation, the market price would go down to $32 or $30 a share (instead of the original $40).

3. If there are corporations with only a few shares of stock sold (say less than 25 shares), lower the market value by ten percent. For instance, if the Royal Corporation sold only 18 shares of stock at $40, lower the market value by $4 to $36 for the next round.

Note: The market value you set is only good for one round. Then you will have to set a new value the next round.

FIGURE 4-11: Formula for Setting Market Prices of Stock Shares. (For teacher's use.)

Debriefing. Discuss such questions as:

1. Did this simulation give you an idea of how corporations are run?
2. Did this simulation give you an idea of how a stock market is run?
3. Were you satisfied with the actions of your corporation officers?
4. How many of you purchased shares of only one corporation? What were the advantages? Disadvantages?
5. How many of you purchased shares of more than one corporation? What were the advantages? Disadvantages?
6. How could this simulation be improved?
7. Could you use this idea when you play your own game of *Monopoly*?

Extensions and variations.

1. A Securities Exchange Commission could be set up to police the corporations and make rules. Any stockholder who was dissatisfied with the operation of his corporation could appeal to the SEC. The SEC could also audit the balance sheets.

2. If corporations increase their net worth by investing their profits, they could be allowed to make stock splits. "Two for one" would mean that each stockholder with one stock share would get two more.

3. Corporations could be allowed to buy shares in other corporations if they wished.

4. The imaginary players could start with a set amount of money, say $20,000 each. When they spent it all, the game would end.

Assignments.

1. Play *Monopoly* with three or four other students, forming corporations and selling stock. Does it make a better game? Did you like it? Report on it.

2. What laws and regulations do real corporations have to follow in selling stock and investing money? Do research and report.

3. What are "mutual funds"? How do they help investors?

4. If you can get brochures from an investment firm, make a display or report on them.

5. What is a broker? What does he do? Report.

6. What is a stock exchange? How does the value of stock go up or down? What makes it go up or down? Report.

CHAPTER **5**

Career Education— How to Make It Lively and Meaningful

A New Curriculum Subject.

Career Education, also called "World of Work," is gaining in popularity as a primary teaching subject in the school curriculum. More states are recommending that teachers include career education at every grade level during the course of the school year. The purpose is to acquaint students with occupations, and give them a view of the working world.

A Drag and a Bore.

For elementary grade students, discussing a career is not an urgent matter. It is highly academic, since it will be years before they can actually begin a career. So it becomes just another dry subject, a drag and a bore, when it ought to be one of the most interesting.

Useless Information.

Much information presented as career education is useless. Who can accurately predict what wage and salary levels will be ten years from now? Who can predict what new job opportunities might come along? Who can predict what present jobs may become outmoded?

An example: Suppose a teacher in 1902 was conducting a course in career education. Some of the important job clusters would include dray making, carriage making, harness making, and buggy whip making. Ignored would be jobs in the automotive, aircraft, radio, and other industries that the students might be working in when they became adults.

What I am saying is that to spend time reviewing each career cluster *one by one* in relation to job opportunities, salary levels, and other facts, is not only boring to elementary students, but unrealistic as well.

Make It Lively.

Something is needed to make career education more lively, more interesting, and perhaps more realistic. That something can be simulations and games.

Simulations Available.

When I did a pilot project using simulations and games in career education (ESEA Title III), I found only a few were commercially available. The board game *Careers* was one. Also there were at that time only a handful of simulations on the subject: COUNCIL, DESIGN, MERCHANT, and POLICE PATROL. (See descriptions in Chapter 10.)

This area of career education is in need of good simulations for elementary and junior high students, and perhaps, using the techniques in Chapter 9, you can develop some good ones yourself.

Games in This Chapter.

I am including five simulations and games in this chapter. One, CONSTRUCTION JOBS, is a simple game using career clusters. Three are for specific careers: REAL ESTATE, SALESPERSONS, and WHEATACRES. One, DOME CITY, is an attempt to predict new careers.

Some of the other simulations in other chapters could also be used in career education. BLUE WODJET COMPANY is one. See the list by subject areas at the end of this book.

CONSTRUCTION JOBS is a board game for up to eight persons. It covers in a broad way some of the jobs in the construction industry. REAL ESTATE is a card game in selling real property, for three to six students. SALESPERSONS is a simulation in buying and selling merchandise, involving the entire class. WHEATACRES is a wheat farming simulation, also involving the entire class. DOME CITIES is a classroom simulation in which students try to predict jobs and careers of the future.

CONSTRUCTION JOBS (a Board Game)

© 1975 by Jay Reese

Resume. This is a board game in which students have jobs in the construction/repair industry.

Teaching objectives. (1) To learn about the qualifications and training needed to enter specific construction jobs. (2) To learn competitive skills in a game setting.

Grade levels. Best for fourth and fifth grades.

Participation. Up to eight students per game.

Time. Up to twenty minutes per game.

Materials needed. (1) Game board (see Figure 5-1).
(2) Set of X cards (see Figure 5-2).
(3) One die.
(4) Money, in denominations of $100, $500, and $1000 (see Figure 5-3).
(5) Eight markers for use on the board—one each, labeled: "Carpenter," "Carpet Layer," "Electrician," "Painter," "Plumber," "Roofer," "Floor Layer," "Brick Layer."

To begin. (1) Players each roll die. Player with highest number goes first, and gets his choice of markers. Second highest gets second choice, etc. There may be only one player per occupation.
(2) One player is the banker.
(3) Each player gets $100 to begin.

To play. (1) First player begins. Note that for the first four spaces all players are to go only one space at a time, and that they may proceed only if they roll the proper number, depending upon their occupation. After the first four spaces, the die number tells how far they go.
(2) Play proceeds in a clockwise direction. Players follow directions on the board.
(3) This game differs from some other games in that players who land on the correct space must pay the other player as directed, whether or not the other players see it.
(4) Game ends when one player reaches last space. All players count money and determine winner.

Debriefing. You may wish to discuss with the class whether they felt this game was realistic, and give reasons.

Assignments.

1. What is an apprentice? How long is a person an apprentice? Write a report, getting your information from an encyclopedia or other source.

2. Write a paragraph about each of the job titles listed on the game board (Brick Layer, Carpenter, Carpet Layer, Electrician, Floor Layer, Painter, Plumber, Roofer). Tell what each person does, and what education or training is needed.

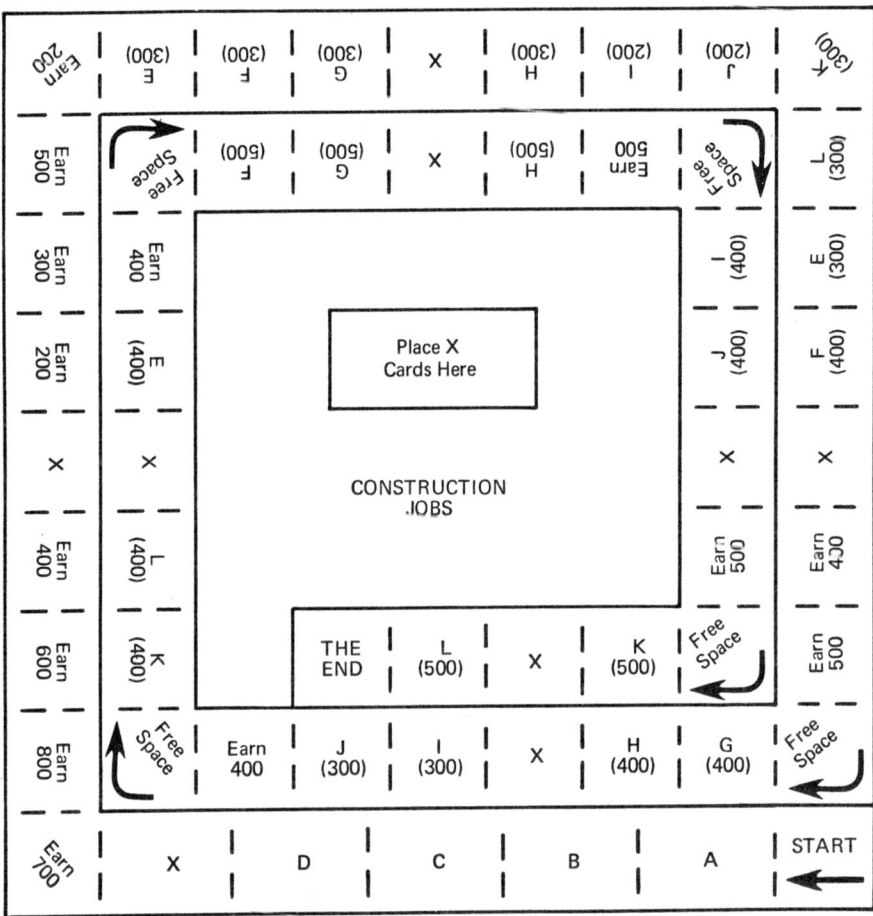

FIGURE 5-1: Game Board. Size is 19 inches square. Spaces (except for first six) are two inches by two and a half inches.

Letters on board refer to below, and what is actually to be written on the board itself.

A - *School.* Roll 1, 2, 3, or 4 to move ahead (everyone).

B - *Apprentice.* Roll 1, 2, or 3 to move ahead. (Roofer, Floor Layer, and Carpet Layer may roll 1, 2, 3, 4, or 5.)

C - *Test.* Roll 1, 2, or 3 to move ahead. (Roofer, Floor Layer, and Carpet Layer move one space without rolling die.)

D - *Set Up Own Business.* Roll 1, 2, 3, 4, or 5 to move ahead. Roll again to see how far. Collect $100 from bank from your first job, before moving.

X - Draw an X card.

E - Pay the Roofer _____ (amount given). (If you are the Roofer, collect from bank.)

F - Pay the Plumber _____ (amount given). (If you are the Plumber, collect from bank.)

G - Pay the Painter _____ (amount given). (If you are the Painter, collect from bank.)

H - Pay the Electrician_____(amount given). (If you are the Electrician, collect from the bank.)

I - Pay the Floor Layer _____ (amount given). (If you are the Floor Layer, collect from the bank.)

J - Pay the Carpet Layer_____ (amount given). (If you are the Carpet Layer, collect from the bank.)

K - Pay the Brick Layer _____ (amount given). (If you are the Brick Layer, collect from the bank.

L - Pay the Carpenter _____ (amount given). (If you are the Carpenter, collect from the bank.)

- -

Note: This game was developed under a Title III ESEA grant. Printed by permission of Oregon State Department of Education.

FIGURE 5-1: (continued): Game Instructions

X CARD Buy a used panel truck and pay $300 as a down payment.	X CARD Repairs on your automobile. Pay $100.	X CARD THEFT INSURANCE CARD Keep this card. If you later draw a card that says your tools, truck, or wallet were stolen, you may turn this in and pay nothing.
X CARD Income tax refund. Receive $200.	X CARD Your tools were stolen. Pay $200 for more tools, unless you have the "Theft Insurance" card.	X CARD Income tax refund. Receive $300
X CARD Weekend job. Receive $100.	X CARD Work for a neighbor in the evenings. Receive $200.	X CARD Your rich aunt sends you a birthday present. Receive $200
X CARD Your tools were stolen. Pay $200 for more tools, unless you have the "Theft Insurance" card.	X CARDS As a bonus for your last job, receive $200.	X CARD Your panel truck was stolen. It was recovered, but damaged. Pay $200 for repairs, unless you have the "Theft Insurance" card
X CARD You need new work clothes. Pay $100	X CARDS Your wallet was stolen. Pay $100, unless you have the "Theft Insurance" card.	X CARD Weekend job. Receive $200
X CARD Buy new tools. Pay $100.	X CARD As a bonus for your last job, receive $200	X CARD THEFT INSURANCE CARD Keep this card. If you later draw a card that says your tools, truck, or wallet were stolen, you may turn this in and pay nothing
X CARD Extra income taxes are due. Pay $100		X CARD Work for a neighbor in evenings. Receive $200

FIGURE 5-2: Set of "X" Cards

CONSTRUCTION JOBS MONEY **100**	CONSTRUCTION JOBS MONEY **100**
CONSTRUCTION JOBS MONEY **100**	CONSTRUCTION JOBS MONEY **100**
CONSTRUCTION JOBS MONEY **100**	CONSTRUCTION JOBS MONEY **500**
CONSTRUCTION JOBS MONEY **500**	CONSTRUCTION JOBS MONEY **500**
CONSTRUCTION JOBS MONEY **1000**	CONSTRUCTION JOBS MONEY **1000**

FIGURE 5-3: *Construction Jobs* **Money**

REAL ESTATE

© 1975 by Jay Reese

Resume. Students are salespersons for a realty company. Their boss has decided to hold a contest to name the top salesperson of the month. For each property they sell, they earn points. At the end of the game, the person with the highest number of points wins.

Level. Fourth through seventh grades.

Teaching objectives. (1) To learn to read with understanding. (2) To experience selling real estate.

Participation. Three to six students in one game.

Time. Thirty minutes.

Materials needed. (1) Thirty-six Option Cards (Figure 5-4). (2) Thirty-six Customer Cards—of a different color than the Option Cards (Figure 5-5).

Getting ready. (1) Prepare the sets of cards. (2) Choose three to six players for each game. (3) Players decide who will begin. (4) Give the players this background information:

> You are all salespersons for a realty company. Your boss has decided to hold a contest to decide who is the top salesperson for the month. For each property you sell, you will receive a certain number of points. At the end of the game, the points are to be added up and the person with the highest number is the star salesperson.

To play. (1) All the Option Cards are dealt to all the players, so that each has the same number. (They will come out even unless there are five players, in which case one card is to be set aside.)

(2) The player who begins draws a Customer Card from the pile, sight unseen. He reads it aloud, and looks at his own Option Cards to see if he has a card that will satisfy the customer. (It must satisfy exactly.) If he does not, each player in turn, beginning with the player on his left, has a chance to see if he can satisfy the customer. If the player who begins (or one of the other players) has an Option Card that satisfies, he places both cards face down in front of him. If none of the players can satisfy the customer (and this may happen, late in the game), the card is discarded until the next game.

(3) The play proceeds with each player in turn drawing a Customer Card, reading it aloud, and trying to satisfy the customer.

(4) When one player runs out of Option Cards the game ends. All the others place their unused Option Cards in the center of the table. All the players count their points on the Option Cards that were face down in front of them. Player with the greatest number of points wins.

(5) At any time, a player may challenge another player's use of an Option Card to satisfy a customer. If there is any doubt, consult the keys shown in Figure 5-6.

Assignments.

1. Clip real estate advertisments from a newspaper and make a display of them.

2. Look through classified advertisements for real estate and choose a home you would like. Tell why you chose it over the others.

3. What are the advantages of owning your own home, compared to renting? What are the disadvantages? Make a report.

4. What is a real estate broker? What is realtor? What are commissions? What is down payment? What is a mortgage? Make a report.

Op 1	Op 2	Op 3
Bedrooms - 1 Age - 2 years Cost - 14.000 Baths - 1 Other - Garage Points - 10	Bedrooms - 1 Age - 10 years Cost - 10.000 Baths - 1 Other - Has a nice, well-kept yard and a garage Points - 5	Bedrooms - 1 Age - 20 years Cost - 10.000 Baths - 1 Other - A big fenced yard, lots of trees. (No garage.) Points - 5
Op 4	**Op 5**	**Op 6**
Bedrooms - 2 Age - New Cost - 30.000 Baths - 1½ Other - Fireplace. garage Points - 15	Bedrooms - 2 Age - New Cost - 25.000 Baths - 1 Other - Carport (no garage) Points - 15	Bedrooms - 2 Age - 5 years Cost - 20.000 Baths - 1 Other - Partial basement. garage Points - 10

FIGURE 5-4: Option Cards

Op. 7	Op. 8	Op. 9
Bedrooms - 2 Age - 10 years Cost - 20,000 Baths - 1 Other - Garage. Freshly painted. Nice lawn; fenced. Points - 10	Bedrooms - 2 Age - 10 years Cost - 18,000 Baths - 1 Other - Nice yard; garage. Points - 10	Bedrooms - 2 Age - 20 years Cost - 22,000 *(includes two vacant lots).* Baths - 1 Other - House needs painting and some repairs. Points - 15
Op. 10	**Op. 11**	**Op. 12**
Bedrooms - 2 Age - 20 years Cost - 12,000 Baths - 1 Other - Needs paint. (No garage.) Points - 5	Bedrooms - 2 Age - over 25 years Cost - 10,000 Baths - 1 Other - Has a huge yard, many trees. Needs painting. Small separate garage. Points - 5	Bedrooms - 3 Age - New Cost - 60,000 Baths - 3 Other - Fireplace; two-car garage; nice lawn; nice view; family room; exclusive area. Points - 30
Op. 13	**Op. 14**	**Op. 15**
Bedrooms - 3 Age - New Cost - 35,000 Baths - 2½ Other - Fireplace; family room; two-car garage. Points - 25	Bedrooms - 3 Age - New Cost - 33,000 Baths - 2 Other - Fireplace; family room; two-car garage. Points - 20	Bedrooms - 3 Age - New Cost - 30,000 Baths - 2 Other - Garage; fireplace. Points - 20
Op. 16	**Op. 17**	**Op. 18**
Bedrooms - 3 Age - 5 years Cost - 25,000 Baths - 2 Other - Garage; fireplace. Points - 15	Bedrooms - 3 Age - 5 years Cost - 22,000 Bath - 2 Other - Garage. Points - 10	Bedrooms - 3 Age - 10 years Cost - 24,000 Baths - 2 Other - Fireplace; garage. Points - 15
Op. 19	**Op. 20**	**Op. 21**
Bedrooms - 3 Age - 10 years Cost - 23,000 Baths - 2 Other - Play room; garage. Points - 15	Bedrooms - 3 Age - 10 years Cost - 20,000 Baths - 2½ Other - Fireplace; garage. Points - 20	Bedrooms - 3 Age - 20 years Cost - 50,000 *(includes 1 1/4 acres of land)* Baths - 1 Other - In suburbs. Separate garage. Points - 40

FIGURE 5-4 (continued)

Op. 22	Op. 23	Op. 24
Bedrooms - 3 Age - 20 years Cost - 20,000 Baths - 2 Other - Dining room; partial basement; fireplace; garage. Points - 10	Bedrooms - 3 Age - over 25 years Cost - 18,000 Baths - 1 Other - Carport, no garage. Points - 10	Bedrooms - 4 Age - New Cost - 80,000 Baths - 3 Other - Fireplace; family room; den; nice yard; two-car garage. Points - 50
Op. 25	**Op. 26**	**Op. 27**
Bedrooms - 4 Age - New Cost - 50,000 Baths - 3 Other - Fireplace; family room; two-car garage; nice yard. **Points - 35** .	Bedrooms - 4 Age - 5 years Cost - 45,000 Baths - 3 Other - Fireplace; two-car garage; family room. Points - 30	Bedrooms - 4 Age - 20 years Cost - 22,000 Baths - 2 Other - Full basement; garage. Points - 10
Op. 28	DUPLEX Op. 29	DUPLEX Op. 30
Bedrooms - 5 Age - 10 years Cost - 18,000 Baths - 2 Other - Needs repairs and paint. Garage. Points - 10	Bedrooms - 2 each Age - New Cost - 45,000 Baths - 1 each Other - Income property; each has own garage. Points - 25	Bedrooms - 2 each Age - 5 years Cost - 40,000 Baths - 1 each Other - Income property; each has own garage. Points - 20
APARTMENTS (TEN) Op. 31	APARTMENTS (SIX) Op. 32	APARTMENTS (FOUR) Op. 33
Bedrooms - 2 each Age - New Cost - 120,000 Baths - 1 each. Other - Swimming pool. All apartments furnished. Points - 50	Bedrooms - 1 each Age - New Cost - 80,000 Baths - 1 each Other - Garages. Points - 50	Bedrooms - 1 each Age - 10 years Cost - 40,000 Other - No garages. Unfurnished. Points - 20
ROOMING HOUSE Op. 34	ONE LOT Op. 35	VIEW LOT Op. 36
Bedrooms - 6 Cost - 30,000 Age - 20 years Baths - 3 Other - Near downtown. Full basement for storage. Furnace. Points - 15	Cost - 5,000 Other - Near shopping district; residential area zoning Points - 5	Cost - 12,000 Other - Nice view of city. Residential zoning. Points - 10

FIGURE 5-4 (continued)

CC 1	CC 2	CC 3
"I want a four-bedroom home, with a fireplace, three baths, and a two-car garage. Price is no object."	"I want to build my own home. Got a lot for sale? I don't want to pay over ten thousand for it."	"I want a four-bedroom home, new or not more than five years old. I will pay between thirty-five thousand and sixty thousand for it."
CC 4	CC 5	CC 6
"I want a view lot, one that I can build my own home on."	"Say, you all, I want a three- or four-bedroom home, somewhere in the thirty to sixty thousand bracket. Y'all got one?"	"I've only got forty thousand to spend, and I want some sort of property with an income. I don't mind working a little bit, like in an apartment house or rooming house."
CC 7	CC 8	CC 9
"My wife and I have ten thousand saved, and we will retire soon. We would like a small house, one or two bedrooms, with a yard for a garden. Got one?"	"We need a house with at least three bedrooms. We can pay only fifteen to twenty-five thousand."	"We own a horse, so we want something near the edge of town, with a house and a little land. We could use two or three bedrooms."
CC 10	CC 11	CC 12
"Say, pardner, got a place where we can bunk in this here town? We need at least three bedrooms and I ain't payin' a cent over thirty thousand. Also, if it ain't got a garage, we don't want it."	"We want a three-bedroom home, with a fireplace and a garage, not over ten years old. We will pay not more than thirty thousand."	"None of these second-hand homes for me. I want something brand new, three bedrooms, fireplace, two-car garage. What do you have?"
CC 13	CC 14	CC 15
"We're getting married next week. We'd like a one- or two-bedroom home. We have money enough for a down payment only on a ten- to fifteen-thousand home. What can you show us?"	"I want to invest in some income property. I would like an apartment house. What have you got for sale?"	"I want to invest in a new apartment house as extra income. Money is no object. What do you have?"
CC 16	CC 17	CC 18
"We want a three-bedroom home, and can pay about twenty to thirty thousand for it."	"We want a new home. We prefer three bedrooms but will take two, as long as the house has a fireplace and a garage. Price? Oh, up to thirty thousand."	"We would like to buy a duplex, so we can have some extra income. We're willing to pay what it is worth. Age doesn't matter."

FIGURE 5-5: Customer Cards

CC 19 "I am all alone, so need only a small house with a garage and a nice yard. I can pay up to twelve thousand for it"	**CC 20** "We want two bedrooms and will pay between fifteen and thirty thousand."	**CC 21** "I'm interested in an apartment house or a duplex. I can pay not more than forty-five thousand."
CC 22 "We can't pay more than forty thousand, and we want at least a three-bedroom home. It must have two baths, a fireplace, and a garage. Can we get one?"	**CC 23** "We have a big family. We need at least a five-bedroom home. Do you have one?"	**CC 24** "I want a good three-bedroom home. It must be fairly new, with a fireplace, a two-car garage, a nice lawn, and a good view. It must be in a good area. I can pay up to sixty thousand."
CC 25 "I would like a two-bedroom home, but can't pay over thirty thousand. I don't mind doing a little work to fix it up. It must be new, or not more than five years old. What do you have?"	**CC 26** "We want a small apartment house that we can live in, and rent out as extra income. We can pay up to forty thousand. What do you have? "If we can't find an apartment house, do you have a duplex?"	**CC 27** "We have three teen-age girls, and need at least a four-bedroom home. We can go up to thirty thousand. Got anything?"
CC 28 "We want to buy a two-bedroom home that we can rent out. If possible, it should have a garage and cost not more than twenty thousand. It should be not more than ten years old."	**CC 29** "I want a home I can fix up some and a vacant lot or two with it that I can build on later. Cost should be to thirty thousand."	**CC 30** "We want a new two- or three-bedroom home, costing between thirty and forty thousand. It should have a garage and one and a half or two baths. Got something like that?"
CC 31 "We want a two-bedroom home, costing not more than twelve thousand."	**CC 32** "We want a three-bedroom home, costing between ten and thirty thousand. It should have a garage."	**CC 33** "We want a two-bedroom home costing about twenty thousand, no more."
CC 34 "I want a *new* three-bedroom home, costing not more than thirty thousand. It must have two baths and a garage. "If I can't find a new three-bedroom home, do you have one not more than five years old?"	**CC 35** "I want a two-bedroom home, costing not more than thirty thousand, and it should be fairly new, say not more than ten years old."	**CC 36** "I want a three-bedroom home, and can pay not more than twenty thousand for it. I know it won't be very new, but I can fix it up."

FIGURE 5-5 (continued)

CUSTOMER KEY		OPTION KEY	
Option Card	Customer Card	Customer Card	Option Card
1.--13		1.--24, 25, 26	
2.--7,13,19		2.--35	
3.--7,13		3.--25,26	
4.--17,20,25,30,35		4.--36	
5.--20,25, or 35		5.--12,13,14,15,21,25,26	
6.--20,25,28,33,35		6.--33,34	
7.--20,28,33,35		7.--2,3,11	
8.--20,28,33,35		8.--16,17,18,19,20,22,23	
9.--20,29,33		9.--21	
10.--13,31		10.--15,16,17,18,19,20,22	
11.--7,13,19,31		11.--16,18,20	
12.--5,12,24		12.--12,13,14	
13.--5,12,22		13.--1,2,3,10,11	
14.--5,12,22,30		14.--31,32,33	
15.--5,10,16,17,30,32,34		15.--31,32	
16.--8,10,11,16,22,32,34		16.--15,16,17,18,19,20,22	
17.--8,10,16,32,34		17.--4,15	
18.--8,10,11,16,22,32		18.--29,30	
19.--8,10,16,32		19.--2,11	
20.--8,10,11,22,32,36		20.--4,5,6,7,8,9	
21.--5,9		21.--29,30,33	
22.--8,10,16,22,32,36		22.--13,14,15,16,18,20,22	
23.--8,36		23,--28	
24.--1		24.--12	
25.--1,3,5		25.--4,5,6	
26.--1,3,5		26.--33,29,30	
27.--27		27.--27 28	
28.--23,27		28.--6,7,8	
29.--18,21,26		29.--9	
30.--18,21,26		30.--4,14,15	
31.--14,15		31.--10,11	
32.--14,15		32.--15,16,17,18,19,20,22	
33.--6,14,21,26		33.--6,7,8,9	
34.--6		34.--15,16,17	
35.--2		35.--4,5,6,7,8	
36.--4		36.--20,22,23	

FIGURE 5-6: Option Keys

SALESPERSONS (a Simulation Game)
© 1975 by Jay Reese

Resume. Students are salespersons, dealing in specific products and services, and customers. The simulation is played twice; the second time, students reverse roles.

Learning objectives. (1) To experience the role of a salesperson competing for sales. (2) To experience the role of a customer dealing with salespeople. (3) To learn how to write checks properly. (4) To learn how to keep a check register.

Grade level. Grades five through nine.

Participation. Whole class.

Time. At least two class periods of thirty minutes each.

Materials needed. (1) Instructions to customers (one per student). See Figure 5-7.
    (2) Instructions to salespersons (one per student). See Figure 5-8 and Figures 5-9a through 5-9i.
    (3) Sales slip forms (ten or more per student). See Figure 5-10.
    (4) Carbon paper for sales slip forms (optional).
    (5) Check forms (five or more per student). See Figure 5-11.
    (6) Check registers (one per student). May be obtained free from banks. See Figure 5-12.

Getting ready. Divide the class into two groups, customers and salespersons. Customers get copies of instructions, at least five blank checks, and a check register. Salespersons each get copies of instructions, and at least ten sales slip forms.
There should be a minimum of the following salespersons:

Two—New autos ⎫ (In smaller classes, there could be
Two—Used autos ⎬ two auto salespersons, each selling
⎭ both new and used autos.)
Two—Life insurance
Two—Sickness and accident insurance
Two—Auto, motorcycle, trailer, boat insurance
One—Motorcycles
One—Campers and trailers
One—Boats
One—Encyclopedias (only in very large classes; otherwise, optional)

(Total, 14 salespersons)

In larger classes, more auto, trailer and camper, and insurance salespersons may be added. This increases the competition.

Students read their instructions and prepare to play.

(In some classes, instructions as to how to write checks and fill out sales forms and check registers may be necessary.)

To play. Salespersons try to get a maximum of sales points by selling to customers. Customers have to choose between competing salespersons. Each follows instructions as to goals and points (see Figures 5-7 through 5-9i).

Simulation ends when all customers have purchased their five items, or at a predetermined time.

Salesperson with largest number of sales points wins.

Customer with largest number of points wins.

Do the simulation a second time, and reverse the roles. Salespersons become customers, and vice versa.

Debriefing. Discuss such questions as:

1. How did you feel as a salesperson?
2. How did you feel as a customer?
3. As a salesperson, did you feel other salespersons were unfair competition?
4. As a customer, did you feel any salespersons were too pushy?
5. Which role (salesperson or customer) did you enjoy most? Why?
6. Which role (salesperson or customer) did you enjoy least? Why?
7. Would you like to be a salesperson again, and sell one of the other products?
8. Did this simulation give you a better view of how sales are made, and of competition?

Evaluation. If you wish to give a test or review as an evaluation, you may ask students to write out answers to the debriefing questions, or you may ask them to write at least five typical problems that salespersons have.

Assignments.

1. Do research upon the products of one of the salespersons (motorcycles, for example). Find out actual costs and selling points.

2. Ask a banker or read to find the answers:

    a. How did checks get started?

b. What are the advantages of using checks?

c. What do the bank numbers and the symbols on checks mean?

d. What does it cost to have a checking account at a bank?

3. Do research upon sales techniques used by salespersons, and report.

4. Find out more about installment buying. What are the terms? How long do you have to pay? What happens if you don't pay? What interest rate do you pay? Make a report.

Note. This simulation was developed under a Title III ESEA grant. Printed by permission of the Oregon State Department of Education.

You have a new job which pays good wages. You will now be able to buy transportation, insurance, and other things which you could not before.

You will start with $300 in the bank, which you can use as a first payment on the items you need. You will have blank checks to make these payments.

You must buy at least five items (you may buy more if you can afford it):

1. An automobile or a motorcycle.
2. Insurance for your automobile or motorcycle.
3. Life insurance.
4. Sickness and accident insurance.
5. One extra thing: a boat, camper, trailer, second car, or encyclopedia set. For all of these, except encyclopedias and boats, you must buy insurance.

You should get the best prices you can on each of these items.

When you write a check, be sure to fill out the line on the check register too, so you will know how much money you have left to spend.

Keep all the sales slips you receive. They are to be turned in at the end of the game, along with your check register.

You will be rated on these points, to determine winner or winners:

1. Completeness and accuracy of check register (ten points).
2. Two points each for each sales slip turned in.
3. Six points for each of the five items you buy. (No points for extra items not needed—like a second boat, for instance.)

FIGURE 5-7: Instructions to Customers

You are a salesperson, trying to make the highest sales for your company. When you make a sale, use a sales slip to write down what you sold, and take a check from your customer for the first payment. Keep a duplicate sales slip for your records. When the time is up, the salesperson with the highest number of sales points wins.

The prices given on your Specific Instructions are for a first payment. When you try to sell, use these sales tips:
1. Be polite at all times.
2. Tell the customer the reasons he/she should buy from you.
3. Do not argue with a customer.
4. Instead of asking a customer, "Do you want to buy this?" give him or her a choice between two things. (Example: "Would you rather buy the sports car or the economy car?") Try not to ask a question to which the customer may answer "No."

Remember, the salesperson with the most points at the end is the winner.

FIGURE 5-8: General Instructions—All Salespersons

You will sell new autos. You can decide what make and model you sell. Your prices for down payments are as follows:

Economy cars, latest models   . . .$80 (4 points for each sale).
    (You can sell them for $70, but you only get 3 points.)
Medium-priced family cars   . . . . $100 (8 points for each sale).
Station wagons   . . . . $100 (8 points for each sale).
    (You can sell them for $90, but you only get 7 points.)
Luxury cars   . . . . $120 (12 points for each sale).
    (You can sell them for $110, but you only get 11 points.)

FIGURE 5-9a: Specific Instructions—Automobile Salespersons (new automobiles)

You will sell used autos. You can decide what make and models you sell. Your prices for down payments are as follows:

Economy cars, one year old . . . . $50 (8 points).
Economy cars, two and
 three years old . . . . $40 (4 points).
Medium-priced cars & station wagons,
 one year old . . . . $60 (10 points).
Medium-priced cars & station wagons,
 two and three years old . . . . $50 (8 points).
Luxury cars, one year old . . . . $70 (12 points).
Luxury cars, two and three years old . . . . $60 (10 points).

You may give the customer a $10 reduction if you wish, but your points will be reduced by one. (Example: One-year-old luxury car, $60—11 points.) Your company does not handle any cars older than three years.

FIGURE 5-9b: Specific Instructions—Automobile Salespersons (used automobiles)

You are a life insurance salesperson. You may make up a name for your company. Your prices for first payments are as follows:

$5000 term insurance . . . . $30 (4 points).
$5000 annuity . . . . $34 (6 points).
$10,000 term insurance . . . . $35 (6 points).
$10,000 annuity . . . . $39 (8 points).
$15,000 term insurance . . . . $40 (8 points).
$15,000 annuity . . . . $44 (10 points).
$20,000 term insurance . . . . $45 (10 points).
$20,000 annuity . . . . $50 (12 points).

Term insurance means that the amount given will be paid upon your death.

Annuity means the amount will be paid upon your death, or will be paid to you after thirty years if you are still alive.

FIGURE 5-9c: Specific Instructions—Life Insurance Salespersons

You are a salesperson selling sickness and accident insurance. You can choose a name for your company. Your prices are:

Dental insurance only .... $25 (4 sales points).
Accident insurance only .... $30 (6 sales points).
Hospitalization insurance only .... $35 (6 sales points).
Medical (doctors, drugs)
    insurance .... $40 (8 sales points).
Accident/Hospital/Medical
    insurance .... $45 (10 sales points).
Accident/Hospital/Medical/Dental
    insurance .... $50 (12 sales points).

FIGURE 5-9d: Specific Instructions—Sickness and Accident Insurance Salespersons

You are a salesperson selling insurance for automobiles, motorcycles, boats, trailers, and campers. Decide upon a name for your company. Your prices are:

$100 deductible trailer/camper or
    boat insurance .... $40 (4 points).
$100 deductible motorcycle
    insurance .... $50 (6 points).
$100 deductible automobile insurance .... $60 (8 points).
$50 deductible trailer/camper
    or boat insurance .... $50 (6 points).
$50 deductible motorcycle insurance .... $60 (8 points).
$50 deductible automobile insurance .... $70 (10 points).
Full coverage trailer/camper or
    boat insurance .... $90 (12 points).
Full coverage motorcycle insurance .... $100 (12 points).
Full coverage automobile insurance .... $100 (12 points).

"$____deductible" means the amount that the insured person pays first on an accident, and the insurance company pays the rest. For instance, $50 deductible means that on a $500 accident, the customer pays $50 and the insurance company $450.

"Full coverage" means the insurance company pays all costs of an accident.

FIGURE 5-9e: Specific Instructions—Insurance for Autos, Motorcycles, Boats, Trailers, Campers

You sell new motorcycles. Decide upon a name for your firm, and what brand of motorcycles you sell. Your prices are:

Economy motorcycles .... $30 (6 points).
Low medium-priced motorcycles .... $40 (8 points).
High medium-priced motorcycles .... $50 (10 points).
Luxury motorcycles .... $60 (12 points).
Racing motorcycles .... $60 (12 points).

FIGURE 5-9f: Specific Instructions—Motorcycle Salespersons

You sell new campers and travel trailers. Decide upon a name for your firm, and what brands of campers and trailers you sell. Your prices are:

Ten-foot trailer .... $50 (4 points).
Twelve-foot trailer .... $60 (6 points).
Fourteen-foot trailer .... $70 (8 points).
Sixteen-foot trailer .... $80 (10 points).
Sixteen-foot luxury trailer .... $100 (12 points).
Economy camper with pickup .... $80 (10 points).
Medium-priced camper with pickup .... $90 (11 points).
Luxury camper with pickup .... $100 (12 points).
Motorhome .... $120 (12 points).

FIGURE 5-9g: Specific Instructions—Camper and Travel Trailer Salespersons

You sell boats. Decide upon a name for your company, and what brand of boats you sell. Your prices are:

Small sailboats .... $25 (4 points).
Larger sailboats .... $30 (6 points).
Economy motorboats .... $50 (8 points).
Medium-priced motorboats .... $60 (10 points).
Luxury motorboats .... $70 (12 points).

FIGURE 5-9h: Specific Instructions—Boat Salespersons

You sell encyclopedias. Decide upon a brand name. Your prices are:

Economy set of encyclopedias .... $30 (4 points).
Medium priced set of encyclopedias .... $35 (6 points).
Luxury set of encyclopedias .... $40 (8 points).
Set of encyclopedias plus set of children's
   books .... $45 (10 points).
Set of encyclopedias plus set of children's
   books, dictionary, and bookcase .... $50 (12 points).

FIGURE 5-9i: Specific Instructions—Encyclopedia Salespersons

SALES SLIP. Make two copies. Give one to customer; keep one.
Name of company _____
Name of salesperson _____
Customer _____
What was sold _____
_____

Price _____   Points _____
Date _____

FIGURE 5-10: Sales Slip Forms

CITY BANK

                              Check number _____
                                      Date _____

Pay to the order of _____ $_____
_____ Dollars.

                       _____

FIGURE 5-11: Check Forms

CHECK REGISTER. Keep a record of checks written, and your balance.				
Date	Check number	Paid to	Amount paid	Balance
Beginning balance				$300
				less
				new bal.
				less
				new bal.
				less
				less
				less
				less
				less
				less

FIGURE 5-12: Check Register Form

WHEATACRES (a Wheat Farming Simulation)

© 1975 by Jay Reese

Resume. Students are owners and operators of dry-land wheat farms. They must decide when to sell their crops for the best prices. They have equal-sized farms. The student with the most money at the end is the most successful farmer.

Number of students. To about 35.

Age/grade. Grades five through twelve.

Teaching objectives. (1) To introduce students to yearly wheat growth cycle. (2) To give students an idea of farmers' expenses. (3) To introduce students to the fluctuating wheat market. (4) To give students an idea of some of the things that affect wheat prices. (5) To give students an experience in the monotonous task of farming.

Materials needed. (1) Wheat bushel cards (Figure 5-13)
   (2) Play money (Figure 5-14)
   (3) Crop insurance lists (Figure 5-15)
   (4) Mortgage forms (Figure 5-16)
   (5) Cycle charts—teacher use (Figure 5-17)
   (6) Squared paper— ¼ inch squares (Figure 5-18)
   (7) Colored pencils, two different colors (optional)
   (8) Legal size envelopes (optional)

To begin. Students are told they are owners of two thousand acres of dry land suitable for growing wheat. One thousand acres are farmed each year, and one thousand are fallow (idle). They each begin with six thousand dollars and twenty thousand bushels of wheat. (These are to be distributed.) Two students are appointed for special jobs, one as wheat buyer and one as banker.

To play.

Round 1 (Year 1). (Each round is one year, but each round may take more than one class period, since eight steps are included.)

Each student is issued a sheet of squared paper. Students are to color alternate squares with alternate colors to create a checkerboard effect. They are to do this as they wait for their turn during the play. This work is to illustrate the fact that much farm labor is monotonous, the same thing over and over again, and also that farmers who work harder usually have better crops. Students may use two different colors of pencils, or a pencil and a pen. These sheets are to be turned in at the end of Step 8 (Harvest), and the students who have completed their sheets will get more wheat than those who have not. These sheets may only be worked upon during the course of the game—no homework or work at other than game time. Students may help one another finish; this illustrates the willingness of farmers to help their neighbors.

Step 1 is Early Fall. Teacher announces the weather (dry), the current market price of wheat ($1.22), and the living expenses that must be paid by each student ($1200). (See cycle charts, Figure 5-17.) All students must pay the living expenses, but may pay in cash from their beginning amount, or may sell some or all of their wheat to the wheat buyer at the current market price.

Step 2 is Late Fall. Teacher announces weather (wet), current market price of wheat ($1.24) and seeding expenses ($3000 cash plus 1000 bushels of wheat). Students must pay wheat and money to bank.

Step 3 is Early Winter. Weather is wet and mild, and current market price is $1.28. Students must pay taxes of $2600.

Step 4 is Late Winter. Weather is cold and wet, current market price is $1.30. Students must pay plowing expenses of $2000.

Step 5 is Early Spring. Weather is wet. Current market price is $1.29. Students must pay miscellaneous expenses of $12,000. (These expenses include interest, labor, conservation, machinery, and marketing costs.)

Step 6 is Late Spring. Weather is good, current market price is $1.28. Students must pay for fertilizer and weed spray, $2000.

Step 7 is Early Summer. Weather is good. Current market price is $1.28. Students may pay for crop insurance, $15,000. This is optional—it insures their harvest in Step 8 against such things as fire and hail damage. Students need not buy it.

Step 8 is Harvest. Weather is perfect. Current market price is $1.23. Any students who have wheat cards left *must* now sell them. (No wheat is to be carried over.) Students must pay harvest costs of $4500.

At the end of Step 8, students receive their yearly harvest. They turn in their squared paper and teacher must assess their work. At least half the class should get the full harvest amount, 35 bushels per acre (35,000 bushels.) Others may get that much, depending upon how much work they did. (Hopefully, the entire class will get the full amount.) Those whose work is below standard get pro-rated lesser amounts (30 bushels per acre, 25 bushels), but no student should get less than 20 bushels per acre.

If, at any step, students are unable to pay their expenses and have run out of wheat to sell, they must mortgage their future wheat crop. The banker will lend them money when they fill out a mortgage form.

Round 2 (Year 2) then begins (see Cycle Charts). It is conducted in the same manner— eight steps as in Round 1. Rounds 3 through 7 are similar.

Teacher may elect to go through all seven rounds (seven years) or may stop when interest grows short. At the end, students turn in all their wheat cards for cash at the current market price, and the student with the greatest amount of cash is the most successful wheat farmer.

Debriefing. After the simulation is over, discuss with the class such questions as these: Did you sell your wheat at the best price each year? Did you learn more about when to sell your wheat as the game went on? How much of the price for wheat is dependent upon things over which the farmer has no control? How does the weather affect crops? Did you always buy crop insurance? Did it help you?

Further suggestions and variations. (1) It may be advisable to pick up all sheets of squared paper at the end of each class period, and distribute them at the next game time. This ensures that students work on them only at the proper times.

(2) Legal size envelopes are of help to students in keeping their wheat cards and money. These envelopes could also be picked up and kept by teacher, especially if there is any chance of students losing them or having them stolen.

(3) Teachers of upper grade students may wish to assign some other work than the squared paper—research, for instance. Research topics might include the history of wheat, the history of bread, the development of wheat farming methods, the changes in wheat farming machinery, and wheat farms today.

(4) Speakers might enhance realism. A wheat farmer or an agriculture extension agent could give the class much background information.

(5) Teachers in upper grades may wish to use actual yearly records and simulate conditions in the early 1900's, in the 1920's, during the 1930's Depression, and so on. Information is included to help in this. (See Figure 5-19.)

(6) In certain areas, such as the northern United States and Canada, wheat is planted only in the spring. The teacher may wish to change the simulation to accommodate this or any other local conditions.

(7) A drought year, with higher market prices but lower yields (say ten bushels per acre), could be inserted.

(8) With some changes and research, this simulation could be used with other farm commodities: hay, sugar, livestock, corn, etc.

Author's notes: The prices and harvest records are actual for the years 1963 (Year 1) to 1975 (Year 7) for Oregon, with some changes for more interest.

Acknowledgement is made to the Oregon State University Extension Service, the Oregon Wheat Growers League, and to the United States Department of Agriculture for information on market prices and average costs.

FIVE HUNDRED BUSHELS OF WHEAT 500 bushels FIVE HUNDRED BUSHELS OF WHEAT	ONE THOUSAND BUSHELS OF WHEAT 1,000 bushels ONE THOUSAND BUSHELS OF WHEAT
ONE THOUSAND BUSHELS OF WHEAT 1,000 bushels ONE THOUSAND BUSHELS OF WHEAT	FIVE THOUSAND BUSHELS OF WHEAT 5,000 bushels FIVE THOUSAND BUSHELS OF WHEAT
FIVE THOUSAND BUSHELS OF WHEAT 5,000 bushels FIVE THOUSAND BUSHELS OF WHEAT	TEN THOUSAND BUSHELS OF WHEAT 10,000 bushels TEN THOUSAND BUSHELS OF WHEAT
TEN THOUSAND BUSHELS OF WHEAT 10,000 bushels TEN THOUSAND BUSHELS OF WHEAT	TWENTY THOUSAND BUSHELS OF WHEAT 20,000 bushels TWENTY THOUSAND BUSHELS OF WHEAT

FIGURE 5-13: Wheat Bushel Cards

WHEATACRES MONEY 100 dollars ONE HUNDRED DOLLARS 100/100/100/100/100/100/100	WHEATACRES MONEY 500 dollars FIVE HUNDRED DOLLARS 500/500/500/500/500/500/500
WHEATACRES MONEY 1000 dollars ONE THOUSAND DOLLARS 1,000 1,000 1,000 1,000 1,000	WHEATACRES MONEY 1000 dollars ONE THOUSAND DOLLARS 1,000 1,000 1,000 1,000 1,000
WHEATACRES MONEY 5,000 dollars FIVE THOUSAND DOLLARS 5,000	WHEATACRES MONEY 5,000 dollars FIVE THOUSAND DOLLARS 5,000
WHEATACRES MONEY 10,000 dollars TEN THOUSAND DOLLARS ten thousand	WHEATACRES MONEY 10,000 dollars TEN THOUSAND DOLLARS ten thousand
WHEATACRES MONEY 20,000 dollars TWENTY THOUSAND DOLLARS 20,000	WHEATACRES MONEY 50,000 FIFTY THOUSAND DOLLARS 50,000

FIGURE 5-14: Play Money

These farmers bought crop insurance for the year _____.

_____   _____
_____   _____
_____   _____
_____   _____
_____   _____
_____   _____
_____   _____
_____   _____
_____   _____

FIGURE 5-15: Crop Insurance List. (For banker's use.)

I, _____, promise to
pay toTHE WHEATACRES BANK the sum of _____
dollars ($_____) at the time of yearly harvest, plus 10% interest.
Date: Year_____, Step _____.
                    Signed:

                    _____

This mortgage note is secured by a crop mortgage upon the entire crop
of the above signee. If unpaid, another 10% penalty is incurred and a crop
mortgage is made upon the next year's crop.
                    Witness:

                    _____ Banker.

(Crop mortgages are given in multiples of $1000.)

FIGURE 5-16: Mortgage Form

Year & Step	Weather	Wheat Price	Expenses to pay.
Year 1 (1968-69)			
Step 1, Early Fall	Dry	$1.22	Pay living expenses $1200.
Step 2, Late Fall	Wet	1.24	Pay seeding expenses $3 an acre ($3000) and 1 bu. per acre (1000 bu.).
Step 3, Early Winter	Wet & Mild	$1.28	Pay taxes $1.30 per acre ($2600)
Step 4, Late Winter	Cold & Wet	1.30	Pay plowing expenses $2 an acre ($2000).
Step 5, Early Spring	Wet	1.29	Pay misc. costs $12 an acre ($12,000).
Step 6, Late Spring	Good	1.28	Pay fertilizer costs $2 an acre ($2000) and pay weed spray costs $2 an acre ($2000), $4000 total.
Step, Early Summer	Good	1.28	Pay crop insurance $1.50 an acre ($1500). (Optional.)
Step 8, Harvest—Get 35 bu. per acre (35,000 bu.)		1.23	Pay harvest costs $4.50 an acre ($4500).

FIGURE 5-17: Teacher's Cycle Charts

Year & Step	Weather	Wheat Price	Expenses to pay
Year 2 (1969-70)			
Step 1, Early Fall	Dry	1.24	Pay living expenses $1500.
Step 2, Late Fall	Dry	1.27	Pay seeding expenses $3 an acre ($3000) and 1 bu. per acre (1000 bu.).
Step 3, Early Winter	Cold & Dry (wheat froze)	1.34	Pay taxes $1.50 an acre ($3000).
Step 4, Late Winter	Wet & Mild	1.36	Pay plowing $2.50 an acre ($2500).
Step 5, Early Spring	Dry	1.36	Pay misc. costs $14 an acre ($14,000), and pay reseeding costs $2 an acre ($2000) and 1 bu. an acre (1000 bu.).
Step 6, Late Spring	Wet	1.40	Pay for fertilizer $2.50 an acre ($2500), and pay for weed spray $2 an acre ($2000). ($4500 total.)
Step 7, Early Summer	Good	1.37	Pay crop insurance $1.50 an acre ($1500). (Optional.)
Step 8, Harvest—Get 35 bu. per acre (35,000 bu.)		1.34	Pay harvest costs $5 an acre ($5000).

FIGURE 5-17 (continued)

Year & Step	Weather	Wheat Price	Expenses to pay
Year 3 (1970-1971)			
Step. 1 Early Fall	Wet	1.43	Pay living expenses $2000.
Step 2. Late Fall	Wet	1.45	Pay seeding expenses $3 an acre ($3000) and 1 bu. per acre (1000 bu.).
Step 3. Early Winter	Wet & Cold	1.57	Pay taxes $2 an acre ($4000) total.
Step 4. Late Winter	Cold & Wet	1.57	Pay for plowing $3 an acre ($3000).
Step 5. Early Spring	Wet	1.00 (dock strike)	Pay misc. costs $17 an acre ($17,000).
Step 6. Late Spring	Good	1.00 (strike continues)	Pay for fertilizer $3.10 an acre ($3100), and pay for weed spray $2 an acre ($2000). ($5100 total).
Step 7. Early Summer	Good	1.61 (strike over)	Pay crop insurance $2 an acre ($2000). (Optional.)
Step 8. Harvest—Get 50 bu. per A. for 800 acres (40,000 bu.)	Good	1.38	Pay harvest costs $6 an acre ($6000).

Other 200 acres lost in fire—collect at current price for 50 bu. per acre (10,000 bu.) if bought insurance. Otherwise, a loss.

FIGURE 5-17 (continued)

Year & Step	Weather	Wheat Price	Expenses to pay
Year 4 (1971-1972)			
Step 1. Early Fall	Wet	1.35	Pay living expenses $3000.
Step 2. Late Fall	Dry	1.38	Pay for seeding $5 an acre ($5000) and 1 bu. per acre (1000 bu.).
Step 3. Early Winter	Dry & Mild	1.39	Pay taxes $2 an acre
Step 4. Late Winter	Wet & cold	1.40	Pay for plowing $4 an acre ($4000).
Step 5. Early Spring	Dry	1.42	Pay misc. costs $20 an acre ($20,000).
Step 6. Late Spring	Good	1.49	Pay fertilizer $4 an acre ($4000). and pay weed spray $5 an acre ($5000). ($9000 total).
Step 7. Early Summer	Good	1.50	Pay crop insurance $3 an acre ($3000). (Optional.)
Step 8. Harvest—Get 55 bu. per A. (55,000 bu.)		1.56	Pay harvest costs $10 an acre ($10,000).

FIGURE 5-17 (continued)

Year & Step	Weather	Wheat Price	Expenses to pay
Year 5 (1972-1973)			
Step 1. Early Fall	Dry	1.87	Pay living expenses $4000.
Step 2. Late Fall	Dry	2.15	Pay for seeding $8 an acre ($8000) and 1 bu. per acre (1000 bu.).
Step 3. Early Winter	Cold & Wet	2.60	Pay taxes $4 an acre ($8000).
Step 4. Late Winter	Wet	2.70	Pay plowing $6 an acre ($6000).
Step 5. Early Spring (Embargo on sale of wheat overseas.) Pay misc. expenses $30 an acre ($30,000).	Wet	1.00	
Step 6. Late Spring	Late Frost (Embargo still on.)	1.50	Pay for fertilizer $6 an acre ($6000). and pay weed spray $7 an A. ($7000). ($13,000 total.)
Step 7. Early Summer	Good (Embargo over.)	2.95	Pay crop insurance $4 an acre ($4000). (Optional.)
Step 8. Harvest—get 30 bu. per A. (30,000) bu.).		3.00	Pay harvest costs $14 an acre ($14,000).

FIGURE 5-17 (continued)

Year & Step	Weather	Wheat Price	Expenses to pay
Year 6 (1973-1974)	(Wheat sale to Russia.)		
Step 1. Early Fall	Dry	4.95	Pay living expenses $5000.
Step 2. Late Fall	Wet	4.88	Pay for seeding $12 an acre ($12,000) and 1 bu. per A. (1000 bu.).
Step 3. Early Winter	Cold & Dry	4.90	Pay taxes $6 an acre ($12,000).
Step 4. Late Winter	Wet	5.54	Pay plowing $8 an acre ($8000).
Step 5. Early Spring	Wet	5.26	Pay to reseed 500 acres at $10 an acre ($5000) and 1 bu. per A (500 bu.). Pay misc. costs $50 an acre ($50,000).
Step 6. Late Spring	Good	4.10	Pay for fertilizer $8 an acre ($8000), and pay weed spray $8 an A. ($8000). ($16,000 total.)
Step 7. Early Summer	Good	4.00	Pay for crop insurance $5 an acre ($5000). (Optional.)
Step 8. Harvest—get 45 bu. per A. (45,000 bu.)		4.36	Pay harvest costs $17 acre ($17,000).

FIGURE 5-17 (continued)

Year & Step	Weather	Wheat Price	Expenses to Pay
Year 7 (1974-1975)			
Step 1, Early Fall	Wet	4.35	Pay living expenses $5000.
Step 2, Late Fall	Wet	4.94	Pay seeding $12 an acre ($12,000) and 1 bu. per A. (1000 bu.).
Step 3, Early Winter	Wet & Mild	4.76	Pay taxes $6 an acre ($12,000).
Step 4, Late Winter	Dry & Mild	4.34	Pay for plowing $8 an acre ($8000).
Step 5, Early Spring	Dry	3.67	Pay misc. expenses **$50** an acre ($50,000).
Step 6, Late Spring	Wet	4.25	Pay fertilizer **$8** an acre ($8000). and pay weed spray $8 an acre ($8000). ($16,000 total.)
Step 7, Early Summer	Good	4.10	Pay for crop insurance **$5** an acre ($5000). (Optional.)
Step 8, Harvest—get 60 bu. per A. for 500 acres (30,000 bu.). 4.50 500 acres were lost in a hailstorm—collect at 60 bu. per acre (30,000 bu.) at current market price if bought insurance. If not, a loss.		4.50	Pay harvest costs **$18** an acre ($18,000).

FIGURE 5-17 (continued)

144

FIGURE 5-18: An **Example of Squared Paper Partially Filled In (centimeter-sized squares)**

PRICES RECEIVED BY WHEAT FARMERS FOR YEAR 1939 to 1965 (see Variations)

Year	Average Price	High (month)	Low (month)	(Year starts with July and ends with June.) Cost of Living (1967 = 100)
1939-40	.71	.76 Feb.	.51 (Aug.)	
1940-41	.66	.80 June	.64 Sept.	1940—42.0
1941-42	.92	.93 Jan	.82 July	
1942-43	1.07	1.15 June	.92 July	
1943-44	1.29	1.37 May	1.17 July	
1944 45	1.38	1 39 April	1.32 Sept.	1945—53.9
1945-46	1.45	1.75 June	1.34 Sept.	
1946-47	1.77	2.16 May	1.69 Sept.	
1947-48	2.19	2.30 April	2.01 July-Aug.	
1948-49	2.01	2.07 July	1.99 Nov., Feb. Apr.	
1949-50	1.98	2.03 May	1.93 Aug.	1950—72.1
1950-51	2.05	2.12 Mar.	1.94 Sept.	
1951-52	2.17	2.26 Mar., Apr.	2.08 July, Aug.	
1952-53	2.16	2.16 Aug., Nov., Mar.	2.12 May	
1953-54	2.07	2.11 Dec.	2.01 Aug.	
1954-55	2.10	2.12 Feb.	2.02 July	1955—80.2
1955-56	1.96	1.99 July	1.94 Sept., Oct., Jan.	
1956-57	2.03	2.31 Apr., May	1.90 July	
1957-58	2.04	2.07 Jul., Aug.	1.89 June	
1958-59	1.81	1.82 Mar.	1.77 July, Sep.	
1959-60	1.80	1.85 Apr.	1.75 Sept.	1960—88.7
1960-61	1.81	1.91 Feb.	1.76 July, Aug.	
1961-62	1.89	1.95 Sep., May, June	1.80 July	
1962-63	1.97	2.04 April	1.92 Oct.	
1963-64	1.90	2.04 Jan.	1.61 June	
1964-65	1.33	1.41 July	1.30 March	1965—94.

FIGURE 5-19: Factual Information

WHEAT BUYER'S CHART, Years 1 to 4. (Round to nearest $50 when paying.)

Price	1,000 bu.	2,000 bu.	4,000 bu.	5,000 bu.	10,000	15,000	20,000
1.22	$1220	2,440	4,880	6,100	12,200	18,300	24,400
1.24	1240	2,480	4,960	6,200	12,400	18,600	24,800
1.28	1280	2,560	5,120	6,400	12,800	19,200	25,600
1.30	1300	2,600	5,200	6,500	13,000	19,500	26,000
1.29	1290	2,580	5,160	6,450	12,900	19,350	25,800
1.23	1230	2,460	4,920	6,150	12,300	18,450	24,600
1.27	1270	2,540	5,080	6,350	12,700	19,050	25,400
1.34	1340	2,680	5,360	6,700	13,400	20,100	26,800
1.36	1360	2,720	5,480	6,800	13,600	20,400	27,200
1.40	1400	2,800	5,600	7,000	14,000	21,000	28,000
1.37	1370	2,740	5,480	6,850	13,700	20,550	27,400
1.43	1430	2,860	5,720	7,150	14,300	21,450	28,600
1.45	1450	2,900	5,800	7,250	14,500	21,750	29,000
1.57	1570	3,140	6,280	7,850	15,700	23,550	31,400
1.00	1000	2,000	4,000	5,000	10,000	15,000	20,000
1.61	1610	3,220	6,440	8,050	16,100	24,150	32,200
1.38	1380	2,760	5,520	6,900	13,800	20,700	27,600
1.35	1350	2,700	5,400	6,750	13,500	20,250	27,000
1.39	1390	2,780	5,560	6,950	13,900	20,850	27,800
1.42	1420	2,840	5,680	7,100	14,200	21,300	28,400
1.49	1490	2,980	5,860	7,450	14,900	22,350	29,800
1.50	1500	3,000	6,000	7,500	15,000	22,500	30,000
1.56	1560	3,120	6,240	7,800	15,600	23,400	31,200

FIGURE 5-19 (continued)

WHEAT BUYER'S GUIDE, Years 5 to 7. (Round off to nearest $50 when paying.)

Price	1,000 bu.	2,000 bu.	4,000	5,000	10,000	15,000	20,000
$1.87	$1,870	3,740	7,580	9,350	18,700	27,050	37,400
2.15	2,150	4,300	8,600	10,750	21,500	32,250	43,000
2.60	2,600	5,200	10,400	13,000	26,000	39,000	52,000
2.70	2,700	5,400	10,800	13,500	27,000	40,500	54,000
1.00	1,000	2,000	4,000	5,000	10,000	15,000	20,000
1.50	1,500	3,000	6,000	7,500	15,000	22,500	30,000
2.95	2,950	5,900	11,800	14,750	29,500	44,250	59,000
3.00	3,000	6,000	12,000	15,000	30,000	45,000	60,000
4.95	4,950	9,900	19,800	24,750	49,500	74,250	99,000
4.88	4,880	9,760	19,520	24,400	48,800	73,200	97,600
4.90	4,900	9,800	19,600	24,500	49,000	73,500	98,000
5.54	5,540	11,080	22,160	27,700	55,400	83,100	110,800
5.26	5,260	10,520	21,040	26,300	52,600	78,900	105,200
4.10	4,100	8,200	16,400	20,500	41,000	61,500	82,000
4.00	4,000	8,000	16,000	20,000	40,000	60,000	80,000
4.36	4,360	8,720	17,440	21,800	43,600	65,400	87,200
4.35	4,350	8,700	17,400	21,750	43,500	65,250	87,000
4.94	4,940	9,880	19,760	39,520	49,400	88,920	98,800
4.76	4,760	9,520	19,040	38,080	47,600	85,680	95,200
4.34	4,340	8,680	17,360	34,720	43,400	78,120	86,800
3.67	3,670	7,340	14,680	29,360	36,700	66,060	73,400
4.25	4,250	8,500	17,000	34,000	42,500	76,500	85,000
4.50	4,500	9,000	18,000	36,000	45,000	81,000	90,000

FIGURE 5-19 (continued)

DOME CITY

Resume. Students write job descriptions for specialized jobs in future dome cities underseas or in space. They then apply for one of the jobs described, and are interviewed.

Teaching objectives. (1) Predicting possible jobs of the future. (2) Learning to write job descriptions. (3) Learning how to apply for such jobs. (4) Learning to conduct job interviews.

Grade levels. Best for grades seven through nine. Will also work for high school.

Time. At least two class periods.

Materials needed. None.

Background information needed. A knowledge of what dome cities are, and of conditions under the sea, or in space, would be helpful. Also helpful would be a knowledge of what job descriptions are.

Getting ready. Discuss with the class the possibility of domed cities of the future, and what new jobs they may provide. These may be cities under the ocean, on the moon, the asteroids, or one of the other planets. Some of the artists' conceptions of what domed cities would look like would make good bulletin board material.

Some of the possible new jobs that could be suggested are:

hydroponics
oxygen supply and control
dome repair and maintenance
air locks maintenance and operation
space suits maintenance
water recycling and supply
waste recycling

To play. (1) Once a list of jobs has been made, divide the class into groups so that two or three persons are together. Give each of the small groups one of the job clusters on the list.

(2) Each small group is to:
  (a) List jobs within the cluster. (For instance, in Dome Repair and Maintenance, there may be persons for Inside Repair, Outside Repair, Ground or Underground Repair, Inspectors, Maintenance Supply, etc.)
  (b) Write a job description for each job listed. It should be as

complete as possible and tell what qualifications are necessary.

(c) Write an advertisement asking for applications for each job. Tell what education or training is needed. Make up an employment application form.

(3) One person from each small group will become Personnel Manager who is hiring for the jobs. The others in each group must leave the group and apply for a job from another cluster (not their own).

(4) Applicants for jobs go to the groups, fill out application blanks, and are interviewed for the job. Of the applicants, the Personnel Manager must choose one person for each job.

Debriefing. Discuss such questions as:

1. Did you feel the list of jobs within each cluster was realistic? Why or why not?
2. Did you feel the job applications and job descriptions for each cluster were realistic? Why or why not?
3. If you were interviewed for a job, did you feel the interviewer was realistic? Why or why not?
4. What could be done to improve the simulation?

Variations and extensions. Instead of having one person from each group do the interviewing, there could be a Personnel Manager (and assistants) for the entire class who could take all of the job descriptions from the groups and interview applicants.

Assignments.

1. Research could be done before the simulation begins as to possible conditions within dome cities, the problems involved in building them, and the reasons for their existence. Or further research could be done after the simulation ends.

2. The simulation could lead to an exercise in creative writing, wherein students would describe their job in a dome city and give a narrative of a typical day at work.

3. Some students might want to draw a domed city, or make a model of one.

CHAPTER 6

How to Use Simulations and Games in Language Arts

The Possibilities Are Great, But Only a Few Games Are on the Market.

Language Arts, since the subject deals with all aspects of using our language, has many possibilities for using simulations and games. But not many are available. There is an increasing number of board games available in the areas of reading, grammar, and spelling. Some of the publishers and distributors listed in Chapter 10 have them. Other areas of language arts have very few. This is a chance for you, the teacher, to be creative and invent something to fit whatever aspect of language you wish to teach.

Ideas for Developing New Games and Simulations, and Blueprints for Using Them.

Some of the areas in language arts in which games could be especially effective are spelling, letter-writing, research skills, punctuation, decoding skills (especially in the remedial area for upper grades), and library skills. You can add to this list as you see fit. If you see an area where traditional teaching does not work effectively, or where students are bored, this is a place for a simulation or game.

Possibly the easiest way to begin is to develop a board game. Or try a simple simulation where students must actually use the skills you wish to develop—punctuation usage, for instance. Chapter 9 gives ideas on how to design your own game or simulation.

Games in This Chapter.

I am including here three types of games that I developed to teach specific skills in my own classrooms. I began AMBASSADORS as an exercise to develop letter-writing skills dealing with a specific social studies topic in the sixth grade. I invented REPORTERS to teach research skills, again using a social studies theme, but it can be adapted to fit almost any topic. STAMP DETECTIVES I created as an exercise in using clues to draw inferences.

In AMBASSADORS, students are United States ambassadors to a foreign nation. They work individually. On their first day on the job, they find in their in-baskets a number of letters, which require answers. Students I taught enjoyed this work, and the letters showed individuality and creativity.

In REPORTERS, students are reporters sent to a foreign nation. They receive periodic "cablegrams" asking for specific news and background information. They work individually, and receive pay for their work. See Chapter 9 for how this simulation developed.

In STAMP DETECTIVES, students work with postage stamps of foreign nations. They try to give as much information as possible about those nations, using only the postage stamps as references. This is also a good activity to use in introducing students to the hobby of stamp collecting.

AMBASSADORS

© 1975 by Jay Reese

Resume. This game may be used in language arts as a letter-writing, creative writing, or research exercise, or it may be used in social studies. Students assume the role of a United States ambassador to a foreign nation. They have arrived at their embassy, and find in their in-basket a stack of letters, which they must answer.

Level. Sixth through tenth grades.

Teaching objectives. (1) To develop an understanding of foreign relations. (2) To develop an understanding of the duties of an ambassador. (3) To give practice in letter-writing skills. (4) To give practice in doing research. (5) To give an opportunity for creative writing.

Participation. Entire class, individually.

Materials and background information needed. *Materials:* Dittoed copies of the letters to be answered, one set per student. (Sample letters are included here; these may be used if you wish.)

Background information. A preliminary briefing on the role of an ambassador may be necessary. (See "Background Material on the

Duties of an Ambassador.") Other information will be needed to answer the letters correctly, and students will need to use reference books.

Getting ready. (1) Give the following instructions, orally or on paper:

> You have just been appointed United States Ambassador to a foreign nation. Upon your arrival at the United States Embassy in the capital, you find mail on your desk, to be answered at once. Write answering letters for each. Be certain your letters are in the correct form. The dictograph machine is broken and your private secretary is on a short vacation, so you will have to write these letters out for your secretary to type when she returns.
>
> Your instructions from the United States State Department are: (a) To foster better relations between the government and people of the United States and the government and people of the nation to which you have been sent. (b) To help United States citizens in their dealings with citizens and government of the foreign nation. (c) To use your best judgment in dealing with other problems as they arise.

(2) Distribute the packets of letters. (In the sample letters presented here we have assumed the foreign nation is Peru, but it would be relatively easy to make up similar packets for another nation.)

To play. This is an individual student project and each student will evaluate and reply to each letter on his own. It will be helpful in many cases to set a deadline for the letters to be turned in, either one by one or as a packet. The teacher's role is primarily that of resource person answering questions and giving directions as to sources of information.

Evaluation and debriefing. How you evaluate the finished letters will depend a great deal upon which skill you are emphasizing. If it is letter-writing, that aspect will be your evaluation. Or it may be creativity. Or research skills. Or perhaps a combination. This will have to be teacher's choice.

The debriefing exercises, if you choose to have them, can be done in two ways. First, each letter may be discussed by the class after it has been turned in. Or the class discussion may wait until the entire packet has been turned in. Questions for consideration and discussion may include:

1. What were the possible ways of answering this letter?
2. Which might be the most realistic?
3. Which did you choose and why?

    4. Did this exercise give you a better picture of the job of an ambassador?

    5. Would you like to work in a U.S. embassy?

    6. What skills would you need?

Assignments.

    1. Find out more about an ambassador and what he/she does. Find out what other embassy officials do: attaches, minister-counselors, counselors, consuls, charges d'affaires. Report.

    2. Make a list of U.S. ambassadors to foreign nations from a current World Almanac.

    3. Find out what treaties are, how they are made, and who signs them. List some important treaties the U.S. has signed.

    4. Find out what it takes to enter the U.S. diplomatic service—what the qualifications are.

BACKGROUND MATERIAL ON THE DUTIES OF AN AMBASSADOR

An ambassador is his/her nation's highest-ranking diplomat (representative) to another country. If from our country, he/she is the personal representative of the President of the United States.

An ambassador is the head of his/her country's embassy in the foreign country. An embassy is the house where the ambassador and his aides live.

An ambassador's duties are:

    1. To conduct communications with the foreign government and its officials.

    2. To look after the political, cultural, and economic relations between the two nations.

    3. To deal with problems of citizens of his/her own nation in the foreign nation.

    4. To direct his or her own staff or embassy officials.

SAMPLE LETTER A

PALACIO DE PRESIDENTE
REPUBLICA DE PERU
LIMA, PERU
(Insert correct date.)

U.S.A. Ambassador to Peru
U.S.A. Embassy
Lima, Peru

Your Excellency:

I welcome you to our country. I am sorry I could not meet you at the airport but I was out of town in the southern part of our county, and shall be gone for the rest of the week. I hope that our Vice-president made you welcome.

I am certain you will enjoy your stay here. You will find Peruvians friendly and helpful.

I hope to invite you to dinner upon my return. In the meantime, I would appreciate your views upon the following questions. Please send your letter to the Presidential Palace and it will be forwarded.

(1) What can Peru offer the U.S.A.? Can Peru continue to sell our copper to the United States at the present prices?

(2) What does the United States have to offer Peru? What products or services can you sell us?

I will appreciate your views.

Very truly yours,

*

President of Peru

*From a current World Almanac the name of the current President can be obtained.

SAMPLE LETTER B

CABLEGRAM.- - - - - INTERNATIONAL CABLE COMPANY - - - - - -
AMBASSADOR OF U.S.A. TO PERU, AMERICAN EMBASSY, LIMA, PERU
  I PLAN TO VISIT PERU SOON IN MY YACHT ON A ROUND THE WORLD CRUISE AND WOULD LIKE TO KNOW WHAT INTERESTING PLACES YOU WOULD RECOMMEND TO VISIT. IS MACHU PICCHU WORTH A VISIT? ARE THE PERUVIANS FRIENDLY? ARE THERE ARE OBJECTS FOR SALE? PLEASE SEND ME ALL THE INFORMATION YOU CAN BY RETURN AIR MAIL. (Signed) JOHN C. GOTLOTSAMUNI, BOX 777, NEW YORK CITY, NEW YORK, 00111.

SAMPLE LETTER C

United States Embassy
Lima, Peru   OFFICE MEMO

To: *The Ambassador*

From: *Receptionist*

Message: *Your mother phoned this A.M., long distance from her home in the United States, while you were out. She asked you to be sure and write her a long letter and tell her all about your first two days in Peru.*

SAMPLE LETTER D

CITY HALL
ACORN PARK, OREGON

Ambassador to Peru
U.S. Embassy
Lima, Peru

Dear Ambassador:

I am writing about having a sister-city arrangement with one of the cities of Peru.

Our great city of Acorn Park has a population of 50,000 persons, and is located in the heart of the pleasant, beautiful, and invigorating Willamette Valley of Oregon. We would like to have a sister city of about the same size.

Could you suggest some cities in Peru that would do for a sister city for Acorn Park, Oregon?

Respectfully yours,

Jim Fattsough

Jim Fattsough
Mayor

jf:jr

SAMPLE LETTER E

P.O. Box 7879-A
San Francisco, Cal.

Dear Ambassador:

I been working in the copper mines and other places in Montana and Idaho and I been hankering for to see other countries.

I been wondering how about chances of working in the mines of Peru. I can operate almost any kind of mining machinery. What are the mines like? Where are they located? Is there a chance for a job there?

I spent some time in Mexico about ten years ago, so I can speak passable Spanish. I saved enough money for the trip.

My writing isn't so good, so I hired a public steno to type this letter for me.

Yours truly,

Harvey Pickacks

Harvey Pickacks

HP:rj

SAMPLE LETTER F

TUBAFOR LUMBER MILL, INC.

1000 Danebo Avenue

Eugene, Oregon

U.S. Ambassador to Peru
U.S. Embassy
Lima, Peru

Dear Sir or Ms.:

I have lots of good lumber for sale, good quality, any width or length. I have also lots of good quality plywood.

What are the prospects for selling lumber in Peru? What's the housing situation there? Are they building new houses? Is there a demand for lumber?

I would appreciate anything you can do to help me **sell** my lumber.

Sincerely,

Ev Tubafor

Ev Tubafor
President

ET:rjw

SAMPLE LETTER G

(Translation of a letter written in Spanish)

North American Ambassador   173 Calle de Perez
USA Embassy   Callao, Peru
Lima, Peru

Your Excellency:

Two days ago, a rich Norteamericano came into my shop and wanted to buy a watch. I showed him some watches and he found one he liked. He asked the price and I said, "Five thousand sols." He replied, "Too much," and offered to pay two thousand sols. We bargained for some time and I came down to four thousand sols. But he refused to change his original offer and continued to offer only two thousand sols. I refused to sell the watch at that price.

He lost his temper, threw the watch to the floor and smashed it with his heel, and then walked out.

I called the police but by the time they found out who he was, he had taken an airplane to Argentina.

What are you going to do about this outrage? Do you North Americans think you can do what you like and get away with it? I demand justice. I enclose a bill.

Respectfully,

/s/ Sr. Jose Kaskaris

Enclosed:

1. A warrant by the Callao Police Department for the arrest of Mike Skinner, U.S. citizen, for "malicious destruction of property."

2. A bill from Sr. Kaskaris for 4000 sols for the destruction of a watch, and 5000 sols for other damages.

REPORTERS

© 1975 by Jay Reese

Resume. Students are American news reporters sent to a foreign nation. They are given specific writing assignments for which they are paid.

Level. Fifth through seventh grades.

Participation. Whole class, working individually.

Teaching objectives. (1) To do research upon specific topics. (2) To learn to organize facts, and present them in logical order. (3) To learn to write complete sentences. (4) To learn to write newspaper copy.

Time. Varies according to topic. In the enclosed suggested cablegrams, twenty-four class periods (days) cover the total assignment.

Materials needed. (1) Copies of cablegrams, one per student. (2) Play money (optional).

Background information needed. Students may need instruction in newspaper copy writing, and the use of the four W's (Who, What, When and Where).

Getting ready. Announce to the class,

> We will pretend you have each been sent to a foreign nation as a news reporter. You are to write news stories and articles for the United States News Services (USNS). Your boss is Mr. Bill Graughler. He will give you assignments and pay you for acceptable news stories.
>
> You will be paid one dollar per word for each news story, if sent on time. If a story is late, you will be paid fifty cents per word.
>
> Each assignment will have a suggested length of words. You will not be paid for less than the minimum or more than the maximum.

After questions about the proposed assignment have been answered, you are ready to begin.

To play. (1) Distribute the first cablegram assignment, clarify any ambiguities and answer questions, and then let the class begin. They are to turn in the news stories when they are completed.

(2) Each cablegram is distributed in turn after the deadline for the previous one has expired.

(3) If you desire, you may pay the students in play money for their accepted news stories.

(4) Caution students they must stick to the assigned subject, and their news stories must be concise and stick to the point—no generalizations.

Extensions and variations. (1) If students are paid in play money, the culmination of the game could be an auction of candy or other items, so they may spend their money.

(2) This idea has been used in American history, asking students to report on news items of the Revolutionary War and the Civil War.

In the case of Civil War reporters, students were to write for either a Northern or Southern newspaper, and frame their news stories according to their audience. They wrote about battles, interviewed leaders and typical soldiers, and wrote editorials.

(3) This idea could be used for reporters sent to any nation. I am using India as an example in the following suggested cablegrams, but it would be fairly simple to use any other nation.

SUGGESTED CABLEGRAMS

Cablegram # 1:

USNS CORRESPONDENT, NEW DELHI, INDIA. SEND INFORMATION ABOUT INDIA. TELL ABOUT ITS GOVERNMENT, POPULATION, AREA, RELIGIONS, CLIMATE, AND SO ON. FIFTY TO TWO HUNDRED WORDS. DEADLINE, THREE DAYS. (Signed) GRAUGHLER, NEW YORK CITY, USA.

Cablegram # 2:

USNS CORRESPONDENT, NEW DELHI, INDIA. SEND INFORMATION ABOUT ONE OR ALL OF THESE FAMOUS INDIANS: AKBAR, ASOKA, MOHANDAS K. GANDHI, JAWAHARLAL NEHRU, RAJENDRA PRASAD. LENGTH, FIFTY TO TWO HUNDRED WORDS. DEADLINE, THREE DAYS. (Signed GRAUGHLER, NEW YORK CITY, USA.

Cablegram #3:

   USNS CORRESPONDENT, NEW DELHI, INDIA. SEND INFORMATION ABOUT THE HISTORY OF INDIA BEFORE THE BRITISH CAME. LENGTH, FIFTY TO TWO HUNDRED WORDS. DEADLINE, THREE DAYS. (Signed) GRAUGHLER, NEW YORK CITY, USA.

Cablegram # 4:

   USNS CORRESPONDENT, NEW DELHI, INDIA. SEND INFORMATION ABOUT THE HISTORY OF INDIA UNDER BRITISH RULE AND WHAT HAP-PENED. LENGTH, FIFTY TO TWO HUNDRED WORDS. DEADLINE, THREE DAYS. (Signed) GRAUGHLER, NEW YORK CITY, USA.

Cablegram #5:

   USNS CORRESPONDENT, NEW DELHI, INDIA. SEND INFORMATION ABOUT THE HISTORY OF INDIA SINCE 1947. TELL HOW INDIA BECAME INDEPENDENT AND WHAT HAPPENED AFTERWARD. LENGTH, FIFTY TO TWO HUNDRED WORDS. DEADLINE, THREE DAYS. (Signed) GRAUGHLER, NEW YORK CITY, USA.

Cablegram # 6:

   USNS CORRESPONDENT, NEW DELHI, INDIA. SEND INFORMATION ABOUT THE TAJ MAHAL. WHAT DOES IT LOOK LIKE? WHY IS IT FAMOUS? WHO BUILT IT AND WHY? WHERE IS IT LOCATED IN INDIA? VISIT IT AND DESCRIBE IT FOR U.S. READERS. LENGTH, FIFTY TO TWO HUNDRED WORDS. DEADLINE, THREE DAYS (Signed) GRAUGHLER, NEW YORK CITY, USA.

Cablegram # 7:

USNS CORRESPONDENT, NEW DELHI, INDIA. VISIT A VILLAGE IN INDIA AND DESCRIBE WHAT YOU SEE. TELL HOW THE VILLAGERS LIVE: THEIR HOMES, FAMILIES, FOOD, WORK, RECREATION. INTERVIEW AN INDIAN VILLAGER. LENGTH, ONE HUNDRED TO THREE HUNDRED WORDS. DEADLINE, THREE DAYS. (Signed) GRAUGHLER, NEW YORK CITY, USA.

Cablegram # 8:

USNS CORRESPONDENT, NEW DELHI, INDIA. OUR AMERICAN READERS LIKE YOUR NEWS STORIES. THEY HAVE ASKED THESE QUESTIONS ABOUT INDIA:
   (1) WHAT WILD ANIMALS ARE FOUND THERE?
   (2) WHO WAS ROBERT CLIVE?
   (3) WHO WAS RUDYARD KIPLING AND WHY IS HE FAMOUS?
   (4) WHAT IS IMPORTANT ABOUT THE GANGES RIVER?
   (5) WHO WERE THE UNTOUCHABLES?
   (6) WHAT IS KASHMIR AND WHY IS IT IMPORTANT?
   (7) WHAT IS IMPORTANT ABOUT MOUNT EVEREST?
   (8) WHAT IS INDIA DOING ABOUT ITS PROBLEMS OF FOOD AND
       DISEASE TODAY?
SEND ANSWERS TO THESE QUESTIONS. LENGTH, NOT LESS THAN TEN WORDS NOR MORE THAN ONE HUNDRED WORDS PER QUESTION. DEADLINE, FOUR DAYS. WHEN FINISHED, RETURN TO NEW YORK CITY FOR PAY. (Signed) GRAUGHLER, NEW YORK CITY, USA.

STAMP DETECTIVES
© 1975 by Jay Reese

Resume. Each student is given a postage stamp of a foreign nation. From it, he/she is to draw as many conclusions as possible about life in that nation.

Level. Fifth and sixth grades.

Teaching objectives. (1) To learn to observe carefully. (2) To use clues in making inferences and deductions.

Participation. Whole class, working individually.

Time. One or more class periods of thirty minutes in length.

Materials needed. Postage stamps of foreign nations, one per student. Stamps with designs and pictures are preferable. The stamps may all be from one nation, or from several nations.

Getting ready. You may wish to begin with a class discussion of how a detective uses clues. He takes nothing for granted, but draws his conclusions solely from what he sees.

To play. (1) Distribute one stamp per student. Tell the students they are now detectives. Using his stamps each student is to draw as many conclusions as possible about the nation it comes from and the life of the people there. No reference books are to be used. The clues will just be inferences or possibilities—they need not be accurate, but they must be logical. Ask the students to (1) list all the writing on the stamp, (2) describe the picture or design, (3) list other clues (postmarks, money, etc.). This will help them draw inferences.

Because each student has a different stamp, some will be able to draw more conclusions than others.

After they have finished, ask for volunteers to show their stamps and read their clues and deductions. Class members may challenge clues or inferences if they do not sound logical.

(2) Once this step has been completed, use a single stamp or enlargement with an opaque projector, and project it on a screen. (See Figure 6-1.) The class as a whole may now participate in looking for clues and drawing deductions. Leading questions about the language, money, ruler, climate, and so on, may spur the class thinking.

(3) After this step, if the interest is still high, re-distribute the stamps (or provide new ones), one per student. This should give

many students the satisfaction of being able to draw more conclusions than they had previously.

FIGURE 6-1: **An example of a stamp illustration (RUSSIA: Apollo-Soyuz Space Orbit), which could be used with an opaque projector, and some possible clues and inferences.**

Variations. Another step would be to allow students to use any reference books they wish and follow up their initial inferences and deductions, and prove them true or false.

Stamps with topics such as Art, Music, Transportation, Portraits, and so on, would be another variation. Rather than look for clues about the nation, students could draw conclusions about the topic itself.

OTHER USES OF POSTAGE STAMPS IN THE CLASSROOM—POSTAGE STAMPS AS TEACHING TOOLS

© 1975 by Jay Reese

1. Stamps can be used in exercises of classification. Singly or in small groups, students can be given a quantity of stamps. They must classify them by whatever logical method they wish. The stamps may be classified or sorted by countries, by size, by color, by language, by monetary system, by topic (illustration), by perforation (the notches on the edges), and so on. This will give students an introduction into the important scientific method of classification. Students may then mount the stamps on butcher paper or tagboard by classification. (Note: To preserve the value of stamps, do not use cellophane tape or glue. Use stamp hinges, available at most stationery stores.)

2. A large number of philatelists (stamp collectors) collect *topicals.* Topicals are stamps issued commemorating a certain topic, or person, or event. Collectors specialize in stamps showing Art, Medicine, Ships, Trains, Bridges, Airplanes, Religion, Science, History, Maps, Space, Winston Churchill, John F. Kennedy, and on and on—the list is endless. In the classroom, students could collect, for display, stamps upon topics of their choice. A timely topic would be the American Revolution. Many United States and foreign stamps have already been issued. Related topics could include men and women of the Revolution. Students could collect stamps showing George and Martha Washington, Benjamin Franklin, Thomas Jefferson, Betsy Ross, and many others. These collections would make good bulletin board displays, or illustrations for personal reports.

3. A stamp newspaper (*Linn's Weekly Stamp News*) has conducted a poll in January of every year. Of all the United States stamps issued the previous year, collectors and others are asked to vote for the prettiest stamp, the ugliest, the most necessary, the least necessary, and other categories. This type of opinion poll could be taken in your classroom. Students could bring United States stamps of the previous year (or they can be purchased at the post office in a set), and one of each design could be mounted on a bulletin board. A vote could be taken, and the results posted.

4. Another exercise is to examine postage stamps as advertising and propaganda for nations. Students may study and discuss the ways nations use stamps to advertise, what types to things or ideas they promote (such as history, scenes to encourage tourism, the arts, famous persons, rulers, national products), and make charts or bulletin board displays with such examples. Upper grade students might find reasons for such actions. Or some nations issue maps on stamps, showing their claims to another nation's territory. Chile and Argentina have issued stamps showing their claims to Antarctica, and Argentina has issued stamps showing its claim to the British Falkland Islands.

5. Some students, in individual research, might want to list and show examples of new and different kinds of stamps. To date, stamps have been issued on gold and silver foil (Tonga, Sierra Leone), in three-dimensional effects (Italy, Canada, Bhutan), on small phonograph records with the national anthem (Bhutan), and in irregular shapes and sizes (Gibraltar, Sierra Leone, Tonga). Stamps have been issued with self-stick adhesives (U.S., Tonga, Sierra Leone). Many stamps (including some from the United States,

Canada, Great Britain, and Germany) have been "tagged" to glow under ultra-violet light to aid in sorting. Stamps have been issued with printing on the back (United States, Tonga, and others). Stamps have doubled as currency (United States, Germany, Russia). Stamps have shown ruinous inflationary periods (Germany issued one in 1923 for fifty billion marks, and Hungary issued one in 1946 for 500,000 trillion pengoes). Displays of these, with research notes, would be impressive.

6. You might want to conduct a stamp show and have students display their collections, and give prizes for the best collections in different categories (U.S., foreign, envelopes, postmarks, etc.). A local stamp club in your city would probably help you in doing this.

Final notes. Non-collectors may think that postage stamps, particularly foreign ones, are too expensive to be used in the ways I suggest. On the contrary, postage stamps are very inexpensive teaching tools. Two hundred different world-wide stamps can be purchased for less than a dollar. Most medium-sized and all large cities now have stamp and hobby stores. Variety stores have hobby sections. And stamps of foreign nations may also be purchased through the U.S. Postal Service, complete with albums.

If you wish to know more about a particular stamp, two major publishers issue yearly stamp catalogs which list every stamp issued to date. Scott's *Standard Postage Stamp Catalogue* is the most common. *The Minkus World Wide Catalog* is also used by many collectors. These catalogs give much information about the stamp and nation, including an average price. The same two publishers also issue specialized catalogs of various nations. Most public libraries have one or both. School libraries should also—though few do.

If students have access to stamp catalogs of various years, they might want to investigate the use of stamps as investments. They could compare catalog prices for successive years and see what increases have taken place. Many collectors do use stamps as investments, and have made money by doing so.

Such classroom uses might start a student on a life-long hobby that would fill his leisure hours with pleasure. With the prospect of ever-shorter working hours, and more and more leisure time, teachers and schools need to do more to give students alternatives to sitting and watching the flashing shadows of a TV screen in their leisure time. Postage stamps in the classroom could thus serve two purposes: to teach, and to introduce students to a worthwhile lifetime hobby. Both uses are worthy ones.

CHAPTER 7

Mathematics Games and Simulations

Many Mathematics Games Are on the Market.

Mathematics seems to lend itself to games. Perhaps it is because teachers recognize the need to combat boredom, and see that they must use other teaching tools and methods. Perhaps it is because students need much drill, reinforcement, and review, and this can be done well through games. At any rate, any catalog of games and simulations will list many mathematics games, mostly of the board game variety. These games cover almost every facet of elementary school mathematics, and every grade level. They cover the four basic operations (addition, subtraction, multiplication, division), as well as fractions, decimals, measurement, place value, money, and negative numbers. Lately there have been many games issued on the subject of the metric system.

On the other hand, while board games are plentiful, simulations are all but non-existent. This also is probably due to the subject area. After all, how exciting is it to pretend to be a numeral?

Yet many existing simulations use some mathematics in their operation. See, for example, BLUE WODJET COMPANY and LANDOSA in this book. Good simulations integrate many subject areas, and thus mathematics is taught incidentally.

Here Are Some That Are Especially Effective.

Even though many mathematics games exist, you can always invent your own to fit a particular problem area in your class, or a particular student.

Here are three games and one simulation, as examples of what can be done.

HOW MANY? is a game which can be done on the chalkboard. I invented it to use as an exercise in estimation, an essential step in doing long division. Long division itself is a complex operation that needs many games for students to use.

YARDSTICK/METERSTICK FRACTION GAME can be used with a yardstick or a meter stick. I have used it to give students more work with fractions. It can be used with two or more students.

MAKE A METER is a game in which students are given varying lengths of paper or cardboard, and attempt to form groups that "make a meter."

COMPUTER SUBTRACTION is a simulation that gives students an understanding of computers and of the subtraction process.

HOW MANY?

Resume. A chalkboard game that involves students in the process of estimation.

Grade level. Fourth through sixth grades.

Number of players. Four to ten students.

Time. Up to ten minutes per game.

Teaching objectives. (1) To learn to estimate in doing long division. (2) To see how accurate estimation can help in doing long division problems.

Materials needed. Chalkboard and chalk.

To play. Students sit in front of the chalkboard so that all can see. The teacher presents a division problem on the chalkboard and asks the first student, "How many do you want?"

The first student must estimate the quotient and give it orally, without using pencil or paper. If the quotient is too large, he loses his turn. If it is adequate, the teacher works out the problem on the chalkboard. If there is a second quotient possible, the second student has a chance to estimate. This continues until the problem is worked out. All remainders are ignored. Then a new problem is presented.

Example. The problem is 165 divided by 22. If the first student should estimate a quotient of 8, it is too large and he loses his turn. The second student has a chance. He says "five." The teacher works out the problem:

$$22\overline{\smash{\big)}\ 165} \quad / \quad 5 \text{ (Jimmy's score.)}$$
$$\underline{-110}$$
$$55$$

The third student then has a chance to estimate how many 22's are in 55. If he or she gives 2, the problem is completed.

$$22\overline{)165} \quad / \quad 5 \text{ (Jimmy's score.)}$$

$$\underline{-110} \quad /$$

$$55 \quad / \quad 2 \text{ (Myrna's score.)}$$

$$\underline{-44} \quad /$$

$$11 \quad \text{(This remainder is ignored.)}$$

The 5 and 2 of the two students Jimmy and Myrna are recorded under their names at the edge of the chalkboard.

At the beginning of the next problem, the fourth child has first chance to estimate. The game continues until all of the students have had three or four tries. Then the scores are added, and the student with the greatest number wins.

To avoid having a student claim the remainder, the question could be worded (as in the example), "How many twenty-twos do you want?" Thus when the remainder, eleven, is reached, students can see there are no twenty-twos left.

This game works well as a review or reinforcement exercise, and may be used with any type of division problem from a simple twenty-seven divided by two to a very difficult one.

As students become more proficient, they learn to estimate as close as possible to the final quotient in order to give themselves a higher score.

Variations and extensions. This game can be led by students who are more able to do long division.

THE YARDSTICK/METERSTICK FRACTION GAME
© 1975 by Jay Reese

Resume. This is two games in one. Children learn about equivalent fractions by using either a yardstick or a meterstick.

Grade level. Grades four through seven.

Number of players. Two to six per game, though you may have as many separate games as you have yardsticks or metersticks.

Time. Fifteen to thirty minutes.

Teaching objectives. (1) To find and use equivalent fractions in a game setting. (2) To become more acquainted with a yardstick and/or a meterstick.

Materials needed. (1) A yardstick or meter stick. (2) 36 cards for each game (see Figure 7-1 and 7-2). (3) Markers. (Not supplied. You may use paper slips, small pieces of colored cardboard, or other small objects.)

The Yardstick Fraction Game.

Object of the game is to be the first to reach the 36-inch mark on the yardstick, moving the markers along the yardstick as the cards instruct, starting at the "0" end.

To play, cards are first shuffled and placed face down in a pile. Players determine who is first, and then in turn draw a card, follow directions in moving their markers along the yardstick, and place the used card, face up, on a discard pile. Winner must reach the 36-inch mark exactly. If, for instance, he is on the 35-inch line, he must draw the "Move Forward 1/12 Foot" card to win. He cannot move forward on any other card, though of course he could move backward if he should draw the appropriate card. Players cannot move backward any farther than the starting point. If the cards are all used before there is a winner, reshuffle the discard pile and use the cards again.

It may be necessary to begin with an equivalency table for younger players, giving the distance in inches. For instance, "1/12 foot equals 1 inch, 1/6 foot equals 2 inches," and so on. As soon as possible, encourage players to work without dependence upon the table.

A large chart-like board could be used in place of the yardstick.

The Meterstick Fraction Game.

Object of the game is to be the first to reach the 100-centimeter mark on the meterstick, moving the markers along the meterstick as the cards instruct, starting at the "0" end.

To play, cards are first shuffled and placed down in a pile. Players determine who is first, and then in turn draw a card, follow directions in moving their markers along the meterstick, and place the used card, face up, on a discard pile. Winner must reach the 100-centimeter mark exactly. If, for instance, a player is on the 90-centimeter line, he could use the "Move Forward 1/10 Meter" to win. If the cards are all used before there is a winner, reshuffle the discard pile and use the cards again.

It may be necessary to begin with an equivalency table for younger players, giving the distance in centimeters. For instance, "1/100 Meter equals 1 centimeter, 1/50 meter equals 2 centimeters," and so on. As soon as possible, encourage players to work without using the table.

A large chart-like board could be used in place of a meterstick.

STAY WHERE YOU ARE	STAY WHERE YOU ARE
MOVE FORWARD 1/12 FOOT. 1/12 FOOT EQUALS ____INCHES.	MOVE FORWARD 1/6 FOOT. 1/6 FOOT EQUALS ____ INCHES.
MOVE FORWARD 1/4 FOOT. 1/4 FOOT EQUALS ____ INCHES.	STAY WHERE YOU ARE
MOVE FORWARD 1/12 FOOT. 1/12 FOOT EQUALS ____ INCHES.	MOVE FORWARD 1/12 FOOT. 1/12 FOOT EQUALS ____ INCHES.
MOVE FORWARD 1/6 FOOT. 1/6 FOOT EQUALS ____ INCHES.	MOVE FORWARD 1/4 FOOT. 1/4 FOOT EQUALS ____ INCHES.
STAY WHERE YOU ARE	MOVE FORWARD 1/12 FOOT. 1/12 FOOT EQUALS ____ INCHES.

FIGURE 7-1: Cards for the Yardstick Fraction Game

MOVE FORWARD 1/6 FOOT. 1/6 FOOT EQUALS ___ INCHES.	MOVE FORWARD 1/2 FOOT. 1/2 FOOT EQUALS ___ INCHES.
MOVE FORWARD 1/6 FOOT. 1/6 FOOT EQUALS ___ INCHES.	MOVE FORWARD 2/3 FOOT. 2/3 FOOT EQUALS ___ INCHES.
MOVE FORWARD 1/4 FOOT. 1/4 FOOT EQUALS ___ INCHES.	MOVE FORWARD 1/4 FOOT. 1/4 FOOT EQUALS ___ INCHES.
MOVE FORWARD 1/4 FOOT. 1/4 FOOT EQUALS ___ INCHES.	MOVE FORWARD 1/3 FOOT. 1/3 FOOT EQUALS ___ INCHES.
MOVE FORWARD 1/3 FOOT. 1/3 FOOT EQUALS ___ INCHES.	MOVE FORWARD 5/12 FOOT. 5/12 FOOT EQUALS ___ INCHES.
MOVE FORWARD 1/3 FOOT. 1/3 FOOT EQUALS ___ INCHES.	MOVE FORWARD 1/2 FOOT. 1/2 FOOT EQUALS ___ INCHES.

FIGURE 7-1 (continued)

MOVE FORWARD 5/6 FOOT. 5/6 FOOT EQUALS ___ INCHES.	MOVE *BACKWARD* 1/12 FOOT. 1/12 FOOT EQUALS ___ INCHES.
MOVE FORWARD 7/12 FOOT. 7/12 FOOT EQUALS ___ INCHES.	MOVE *BACKWARD* 1/3 FOOT. 1/3 FOOT EQUALS ___ INCHES.
MOVE FORWARD 5/12 FOOT. 5/12 FOOT EQUALS ___ INCHES.	MOVE *BACKWARD* 1/6 FOOT. 1/6 FOOT EQUALS ___ INCHES.
MOVE FORWARD 1/3 FOOT. 1/3 FOOT EQUALS ___ INCHES.	MOVE *BACKWARD* 1/4 FOOT. 1/4 FOOT EQUALS ___ INCHES.
MOVE FORWARD 1/3 FOOT. 1/3 FOOT EQUALS ___ INCHES.	MOVE *BACKWARD* 1/12 FOOT. 1/12 FOOT EQUALS ___ INCHES.
MOVE FORWARD 3/4 FOOT. 3/4 FOOT EQUALS ___ INCHES.	MOVE *BACKWARD* 1/6 FOOT. 1/6 FOOT EQUALS ___ INCHES.

FIGURE 7-1 (continued)

STAY WHERE YOU ARE	STAY WHERE YOU ARE.
MOVE FORWARD 1/100 METER. 1/100 METER EQUALS ____ CM.	MOVE FORWARD 1/50 METER. 1/50 METER EQUALS ____ CM.
MOVE FORWARD 1/50 METER. 1/50 METER EQUALS ____ CM.	MOVE FORWARD 1/100 METER. 1/100 METER EQUALS ____ CM.
MOVE FORWARD 1/100 METER. 1/100 METER EQUALS ____ CM.	STAY WHERE YOU ARE.
STAY WHERE YOU ARE.	MOVE FORWARD 1/50 METER. 1/50 METER EQUALS ____ CM.
MOVE FORWARD 1/100 METER. 1/100 METER EQUALS ____ CM.	MOVE FORWARD 1/50 METER. 1/50 METER EQUALS ____ CM.

FIGURE 7-2: Cards for the Meterstick Fraction Game

MOVE FORWARD 1/5 METER. 1/5 METER EQUALS ____ CM.	MOVE FORWARD 3/10 METER. 3/10 METER EQUALS ____ CM.
MOVE FORWARD 3/10 METER. 3/10 METER EQUALS ____ CM.	MOVE FORWARD 1/5 METER. 1/5 METER EQUALS ____ CM.
MOVE FORWARD 1/10 METER. 1/10 METER EQUALS ____ CM.	MOVE FORWARD 1/50 METER. 1/50 METER EQUALS ____ CM.
MOVE FORWARD 1/10 METER. 1/10 METER EQUALS ____ CM.	MOVE FORWARD 1/4 METER. 1/4 METER EQUALS ____ CM.
MOVE FORWARD 1/5 METER. 1/5 METER EQUALS ____CM.	MOVE FORWARD 1/10 METER. 1/10 METER EQUALS ____ CM.
MOVE FORWARD 1/10 METER. 1/10 METER EQUALS ____ CM.	MOVE FORWARD 1/100 METER. 1/100 METER EQUALS ____ CM.

FIGURE 7-2 (continued)

MOVE FORWARD 3/10 METER. 3/10 METER EQUALS ____ CM.	MOVE FORWARD 1/4 METER. 1/4 METER EQUALS ____ CM.
MOVE FORWARD 1/10 METER. 1/10 METER EQUALS ____ CM.	MOVE FORWARD 1/5 METER. 1/5 METER EQUALS ____ CM.
MOVE FORWARD 2/5 METER. 2/5 METER EQUALS ____ CM.	MOVE *BACKWARD* 1/100 METER. 1/100 METER EQUALS ____ CM.
MOVE *BACKWARD* 1/50 METER. 1/50 METER EQUALS ____ CM.	MOVE *BACKWARD* 1/10 METER. 1/10 METER EQUALS ____ CM.
MOVE FORWARD 1/4 METER. 1/4 METER EQUALS ____ CM.	MOVE *BACKWARD* 1/5 METER. 1/5 METER EQUALS ____ CM.
MOVE *BACKWARD* 1/50 METER. 1/50 METER EQUALS ____ CM.	MOVE *BACKWARD* 1/100 METER. 1/100 METER EQUALS ____ CM.

FIGURE 7-2 (continued)

MAKE A METER

Resume. Students are given varying lengths of cardboard. They try to join others and make a meter in length.

Number of students. Any number.

Teaching objectives. (1) To learn to estimate the length of a meter. (2) To learn to work cooperatively.

Materials. Strips of tagboard or other type of cardboard, at least thirty centimeters long and the width of an average ruler. Cut two per student. Meter sticks are also needed, one for about every four students.

Getting ready. Mark varying line segments on the strips of tagboard. These line segments should be decimeter length, and one line segment should be drawn on each strip. The strips should be roughly divided between the following lengths: one decimeter, two decimeters, three decimeters, one and a half decimeters.

Directions for play. Give each student one strip of tagboard, at random.

Students are to be directed to walk around and try to find others to join, so that a group will have a total of one meter in length if all the line segments are placed end to end.

When a group thinks it has a meter, all members sit down.

After five minutes, or when all or almost all students are in groups, let each group measure against a meter stick. (Once they have started to measure, no one else may join the group.)

The group that is the nearest to a meter in length is the winner. It doesn't matter whether they are over or short.

Collect all the strips, and if time (and student interest) allows, distribute them again, and go through the same procedure. The reason for a second game is to let students who may have been left out of the first one have a chance to join a group.

Variations.

1. Give each student two strips and let them try to form groups. Each student must use both strips to form a meter.

2. Make strips with smaller segments: two centimeters, four centimeters, six centimeters, eight centimeters. Use these after the students have become proficient with the larger segments.

COMPUTER SUBTRACTION

Resume. Students simulate, in a simple way, the action of a computer (or calculator) in doing base-ten subtraction. They compete in teams, doing subtraction problems.

Time. One-half hour or more.

Grade levels. Fourth through seventh grades.

Number of students. Eight or more.

Teaching objectives. (1) To enable students to understand the steps in subtracting. (2) To give students a simple understanding of how a computer works.

Materials. (1) Blank 3 x 5 cards, about twenty per team of eight students. (2) Pencils and paper, one per student. (3) Dittoed directions. (See "Directions for Teams.")

Setting up. Divide the class into teams of eight students each. Extra students will have to watch (though you could have smaller teams by having one student on each team do more than one operation).

To play. (1) Tell the students, "You are now parts of a computer. You will be given instructions as to what to do, and then the teams will compete against each other in doing subtraction problems. The fastest team wins."

(2) Hand out the cards, and the individual directions.

(3) Seat teams of students in a row, so that A is first, and H last.

(4) After individuals on each team have had a chance to study their directions, give a four-digit subtraction problem to student A on each team, and then say "Go."

(5) The team that completes the problem correctly first is the winner.

(6) In order to give students an understanding of the subtraction process, play the game several times. But each time, have members of each team exchange places (for instance, A goes to H, B to A, C to B, etc.).

Variations and extensions. (1) Use different number bases when students understand the process, base six for example. Either give the beginning problem in that number base, or have additional students in each team convert that base to base ten as initial steps. Then have others convert the answer back to the original base (in this case base six).

(2) Try your hand at using this system with addition, multiplication, or even division. Instructions would have to be changed. Keep the steps simple.

(3) You could use this subtraction system with metric units—327.9 meters less 274.8 meters, for instance.

DIRECTIONS FOR TEAMS

(Letters refer to team members. Ditto these directions, cut them apart, and give each letter to the particular member of each team.)

A. You will receive a subtraction problem. You are to write the minuend (top number) on one card and give it to B. You are to write the subtrahend (bottom number) on another card and give it to C.

B. You will receive a card from A. You are to use the number on the card and write it in expanded notation form. (Example: 3247 = 3000 + 200 + 40 + 7.) Then write the ones number on the first card, and give it to D (mark it *minuend*). Write the tens number on a second card (write the word *minuend* on the card also) and give it to E. Write the hundreds number on a third card (write *minuend* on the card) and give it to F. Write the thousands number on a fourth card (write *minuend*) and give it to G.

C.   You will receive a card from A. You are to use the number on the card and write it in expanded notation form. (Example: 2998 = 2000 + 900 + 90 + 8.) Then write the ones number on the first card (also write the word *subtrahend* on the card) and give it to D. Write the tens number on a second card (also the word *subtrahend*) and give it to E. Write the hundreds number on a third card (also the word *subtrahend*) and give it to F. Write the thousands number on a fourth card (also the word *subtrahend*) and give it to G.

D.   You will receive two cards with numbers on them. One will be marked "minuend" and one "subtrahend." Ask yourself, "Will the subtrahend subtract from the minuend?"

   If your answer is "Yes," subtract it and hand the answer on a card to H. Also give a card to E, saying YES.

   If your answer is "No," you must get ten more ones from E. Give E a card saying "Give me one more ten." Then add ten to the minuend, and subtract. Give the answer on a card to H.

E.   You will receive two cards with numbers on them. One will be marked "minuend" and one "subtrahend." Do nothing until you receive a card from D. The card will either say "Yes" or "Give me one more ten."

   If the card says "Give me one more ten," subtract a ten from your minuend. Then go on to the "Yes" step.

   If the card says "Yes," ask yourself, "Will the subtrahend subtract from the minuend?"

   If your answer is "Yes," subtract it and hand the answer on a card to H. Also give a card to F saying YES.

   If your answer is "No," give a card to F saying "Give me one more hundred." Add a hundred to the minuend, and then subtract. Give the answer to H.

F. You will receive two cards with numbers on them. One will be marked "minuend" and one "subtrahend." Do nothing until you receive a card from E. The card will either say "Yes" or "Give me one more hundred."

If the card says "Give me one more hundred," subtract a hundred from your minuend. Then go on to the "Yes" step.

If the card says "Yes," ask yourself, "Will the subtrahend subtract from the minuend?"

If your answer is "Yes," subtract it and hand the answer on a card to H. Also give a card to G saying "Yes."

If your answer is "No," give a card to G saying "Give me one more thousand." Add a thousand to the minuend, and then subtract. Give the answer to H.

G. You will receive two cards with numbers on them. One will be marked "minuend" and one "subtrahend." Do nothing until you receive a card from F. The card will either say "Yes," or "give me one more thousand."

If the card says "Give me one more thousand," subtract a thousand from your minuend. Then go on to the "Yes" step.

If the card says "Yes," subtract it and hand the answer on a card to H.

H. You will receive four cards with numbers on them. Add the four numbers. Put the total on another card. Hold up your hand with the card (with the answer on it) to show your group is finished.

CHAPTER 8

Simulations and Games in Other Key Subject Areas

Other Curriculum Areas Can Be Taught
By Using Simulations and Games.

In addition to the curriculum areas given in separate chapters in this book, there are others in which simulations and games can be used to an advantage.

Computer Simulations.

A number of simulations have been programed for use in a computer. Most of these so far are for high school and adult use, but a few may be used in the upper elementary grades, especially with mature students. As computer terminals become more common in elementary schools, this type of simulation will have more use. It is a good method for single students or for small groups. It doesn't work well for large groups, or anything requiring group interaction, except to a limited extent. Brighter students who need extra challenges and extra work would benefit a great deal by using computer simulations. A simulation such as BLUE WODJET COMPANY given in this book could be programed into a computer very easily, and the student could do the simulation a second or third time and try other decisions to see where they led.

Simulations in Chapter 8.

The simulations given in this chapter are VOYAGEURS, SPICE TRADE, and INFLUENCE.

VOYAGEURS involves geography and history. It covers the historic period of the fur-trading companies, and the discovery and exploitation of fur-trade areas.

SPICE TRADE involves history and geography also. It covers the time when Europeans were in need of spices and explored new ways of reaching the spice sources. It gives students a better understanding of why Columbus sailed west, as they too try to find an alternate route to get spices.

INFLUENCE takes up the topic of class interaction and how students are influenced by (or attempt to influence) their classmates.

VOYAGEURS

Resume. Students are members of trading companies hunting for furs and competing for fur-trading areas.

Number of players. From ten to about thirty.

Grade levels. Fourth, fifth, and sixth grades.

Teaching objectives. (1) To understand the fur-trading era in North America. (2) To understand the rivalry between historic fur companies. (3) To experience the thrills of discovery.

Materials needed. (1) Large bulletin board grid (see Figure 8-1). (2) Colored map pins, one for each group (six to ten colors). (3) Forms 1 and 2, dittoed, one for each group.

Setting up. (1) Choose the groups which will simulate fur-trading companies. There may be two to five persons per group.

(2) Each company must choose a name and sign a charter form.

(3) Put up the bulletin board grid map.

(4) Assign a colored map pin for each group.

To play. (1) Give the students the following background information:

> You are now members of fur-trading companies that are setting out to explore an unknown land, find fur areas, and build forts and factories. (Directors and leaders of your company are called "factors" and thus the places where they live are called "factories.") Your colored map pin will represent your explorer group.

(2) Read or explain the following Rules of Play:

> Each company will start from a seaport (Charlesport or Newsea). The companies take turns moving. They may move each turn upstream or across level land. They may move two squares each turn downstream. They may move one-half square a turn over mountains,

or around a portage. If they want to build a factory, they must stop a turn. If they want to build a fort, they must stop two turns.

Each company must by the end of the game have one fort (the home base), one factory located along a river or body of water in each fur-producing area, and a trail from each factory to their home fort and from the home fort to Charlesport.

Each company may name the lakes, rivers, falls, and so on, discovered.

Each company need only to enter a fur-bearing area to claim it, but in order to have exclusive control over the area it must all be explored. Thus if one company claims a fur-producing area, but has not explored it all, another company may come in and explore part and have a claim to that part.

Disputed areas may be divided between the companies by mutual agreement. If the companies cannot agree, the King or Queen (teacher) is the arbitrator, for a fee of 25%.

At the end, points are awarded to each company as follows, and the company with the most points wins:

1. One point for each fur-producing square claimed.
2. Two points for each factory (there can be only one factory per area).
3. Three points for each fort (there can be only one per company).
4. One point for each trail.
5. Subtract one point each if there is no trail, or factory, or fort.

(3) Teacher: As the companies progress on the map, draw in the features indicated on the small master map (Figure 8-2). Trails by the companies may be drawn in in colored pen or pencil.

Debriefing. Discuss the strategies involved. Also see if students can put into words what it felt like to be an explorer.

Extensions and variations.

1. Have all students work for one company and give points for discoveries and exploration only.
2. Have half the companies be from another nation, competing like the Hudson's Bay Company and Astor's American Fur Company.

Assignments.

1. Compare the simulated explorations to the actual explorations of persons in the Hudson's Bay Company.
2. Look up some of the early trappers and fur traders and make reports on them.

3. Look up the origin of the word *voyageurs* and report on it.

4. On a map of North America, place the actual forts and trails for the different fur companies.

5. Find out why there was such a demand for furs at this time, particularly beaver. What made beaver so expensive?

WE, KING CHARLES, do hereby grant to the undersigned gentlemen and lady adventurers, this Royal Charter.

(signed)

(Seal)

Charles VII, King.

We, the undersigned gentlemen and lady adventurers, do form a company to be known as _____

for the purpose of exploration and fur trade. All land found shall remain the property of His Majesty King Charles, except certain forts and factories maintained by said company. All profits shall be shared equally.

Date: Signed:

FORM 1: Voyageurs. ROYAL CHARTER

We, the undersigned, representing the companies of _____

_____ and _____, do agree to share the fur-bearing area known as _____. We will divide the furs from this area on a _____ basis.

(signed)

Date:

FORM 2: Voyageurs. AGREEMENT

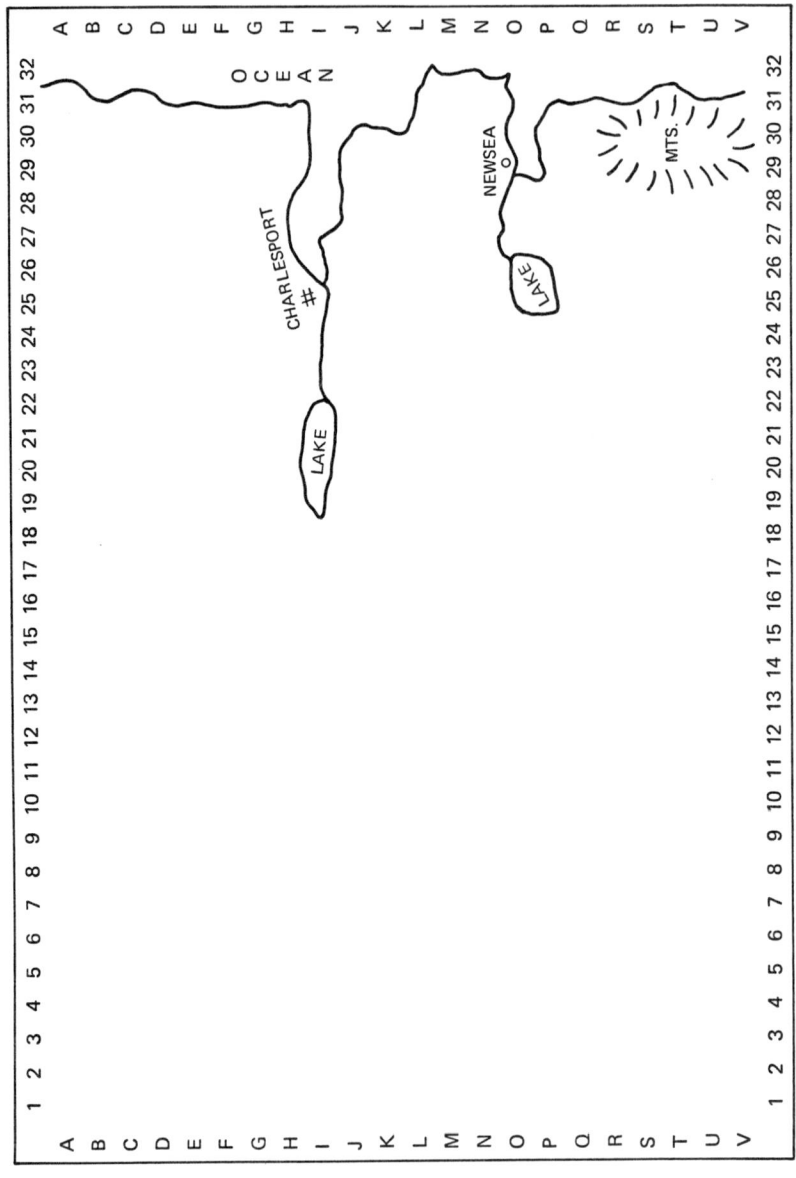

FIGURE 8-1: Bulletin Board Map. Fill in only what is shown on this map. ENLARGE
THIS MAP TWO OR THREE TIMES THE PRESENT SIZE.

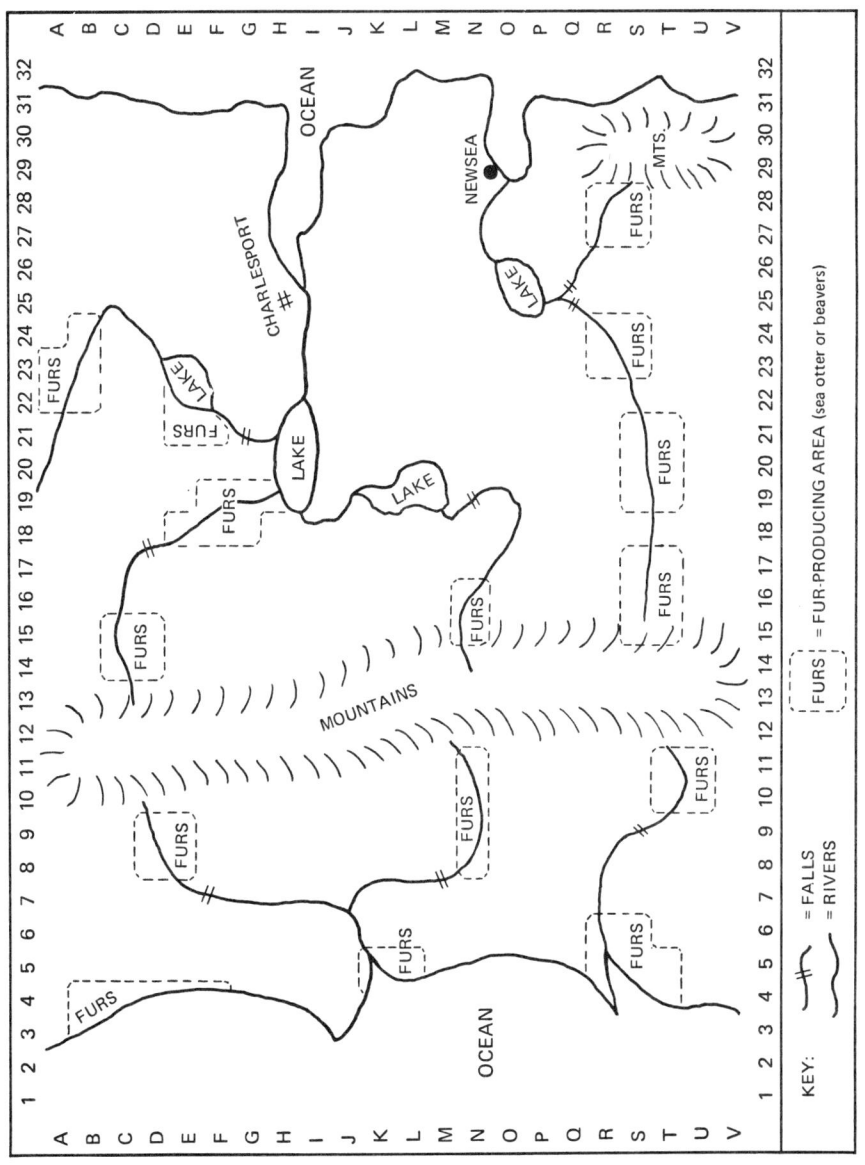

FIGURE 8-2: Master Teacher Map. Fill in details from this map on the bulletin board map as companies move.

KEY: ⊣⊢ = FALLS

⌇ = RIVERS

⌐FURS¬ = FUR-PRODUCING AREA (sea otter or beavers)

189

SPICE TRADE
© 1975 by Jay Reese

Resume. Students are buyers and sellers of spices during the time of Columbus. In the first round, buyers combine their assets, form companies, buy ships and trading goods. They sail to the Spice Islands, buy spices from sellers, and return home (if they are lucky). In the second round, a barrier is placed between buyers and sellers and buyers must find another way of reaching the Spice Islands (i.e., "around the world").

Grade levels. Fourth through seventh grades.

Time. At least two class periods of thirty to forty-five minutes each, though one longer class period of about an hour will do.

Teaching objectives. (1) To enable students to see why Columbus felt it was so important to reach India. (2) To give students an experience in problem-solving. (3) To enable students to appreciate the dangers (and opportunities) in spice trading during the time of Columbus.

Materials needed. (1) Money (Figure 8-3). (2) Flavored toothpicks, at least three per student. You may buy pre-flavored toothpicks, or soak round toothpicks in a spice extract or oil and then dry on paper towels. (For alternatives to toothpicks, see Variation 2, below.) (3) Ship cards (Figure 8-4). (4) Trading Goods cards (Figure 8-5). (5) Travel Hazards cards (Figure 8-6). (6) Rope or string, classroom-length.

To set up. In setting up SPICE TRADE in a typical classroom, an arrangement similar to the one shown in Figure 8-7 has proven best.

First read and discuss the Background Material for Students. (The material may be dittoed and distributed if you wish.) Then divide the students into two groups. A small group (about one-fourth of the class or no less than four students) are specialty persons. Two or more are spice sellers. They go to a corner of the room near a window or near a second door and are given the flavored toothpicks. One student is the shipbuilder with the Ship cards, and one student is the ship outfitter with the Trading Goods cards. These two go to a central place in the room.

The second, larger group are spice buyers. Each student in the second group is given one hundred ducats in play money.

To play.

Round 1. Students in the spice buyers group informally form trading groups (partnerships of three or more students) and each trading group must buy at least one ship and one shipload of trading goods. Ships cost two hundred ducats each and a shipload of trading goods costs fifty ducats. Each group chooses a leader, the captain. They may choose names for their ships if they wish.

The loaded ships then set sail. Each group leader (ship captain) must now draw a Travel Hazard card to see if the ship arrives safely.

If the ship arrives safely, the captain takes the Ship card and Trading Goods card to the spice sellers, and trades the cargo for ten toothpicks.

Each captain who has made a trade must then draw another Travel Hazard card to see if the ship arrives safely home.

After the ship arrives safely home, the group partners may share the toothpicks any way they wish. All trading groups of all ships that arrive home safely with their toothpicks are winners of this round.

Round 2. The same trading groups and same ships are used. Before the round begins, tie the rope or string between two chairs so that the trading groups and spice sellers are separated, and so that the trading groups (buyers) have at least one classroom exit door they may use. Announce that this is an "impassable barrier" and no one may cross it, go around it, or trade across it.

Then give the members of the winning trading groups from Round 1 each five hundred ducats. Students from the unsuccessful trading groups are given one hundred ducats each.

The trading groups now buy new ships and cargoes as needed. They must try again to trade for spice, with the understanding that they cannot cross the barrier in any manner. The buyers must somehow figure out an alternate route to use to get to the spice sellers. It may be out one classroom door and in another. It may be out a classroom door and in a window. If the classroom is on a second floor and has only one door, then if students can tell you how they *could* make the trip (like climbing a fire escape), they need not physically do it. They may pretend they have made the trip, and cross the barrier to the spice sellers.

Once the route is established, use the same steps (Travel Hazard card, arrival, trading, Travel Hazard card, home) as in Round 1.

The trading groups that arrive home safely are the winners of this round.

Debriefing. Discuss with the class such questions as:

1. Did your group have a safe voyage either time?
2. If you did not, do you think traveling in the days of Columbus was safe?
3. Could you see what the use of the barrier meant?
4. Were you successful in finding an alternate route?
5. Did you begin to feel like a spice merchant, or like Columbus?

Variations and extensions.

Variation 1: Give the spice buyers only fifty ducats each, and have a Queen (or King) with money to loan, for a percentage of the profits.

Variation 2: Use something other than toothpicks. You could use tiny bags of spices, or wrapped candies, or candied ginger, or whole cloves, or cards labeled "Spices," for instance.

Variation 3: Allow students to cross the "impassable barrier" by paying a bribe of five hundred or a thousand ducats.

Extension 1: Play *Explorers 1* or *Explorers 2* (from SIMILE II).

Assignments.

1. Collect samples of an many different kinds of spices as you can. Display them on a bulletin board or put them in a booklet. Label each one.

2. Put samples of spices on a bulletin board, unlabeled, and ask your classmates if they can identify them.

3. Find out where different spices are grown nowadays, and make a report.

4. Read about voyages during Columbus' time, and draw the routes on a map.

5. List the explorers of the 1400's and 1500's and what they found.

BACKGROUND MATERIAL FOR STUDENTS

Around the time of Columbus in Europe, spices became very important in cooking. Since early times, man had preserved meat by drying or salting it. But these methods changed the flavor. When merchants from cities like Venice began to trade with the East, spice came into use. Meat was heavily spiced as it was kept, and the flavor of decay was disguised with spices. More people could eat meat more often. Food tasted better.

Spices like cloves, cinnamon, pepper, nutmeg, and ginger could be obtained only in the tropics. India and the nearby islands (the Moluccas or Spice Island, Ceylon, and some of the East Indies) were the most common sources.

For a long time, merchants could obtain these spices only by a long land and water trip across the Middle East. They made great profits from even a single successful trip. But this route was long and dangerous and after a time it was closed by unfriendly people.

So an alternate route to the spices had to be found. Columbus was not really trying to prove the world was round (many scholars of his day believed that). But he was trying to find an all-water route to India where he could get spices. (He thought at first he had made it, which is why he called the people he found "Indians.") Other explorers, mainly from Portugal, were trying at the same time to sail around Africa. Even after the discovery of the New World, explorers still tried to find a route around North and South America to the Spice Islands. Some Dutch and English Explorers searched for a "Northwest Passage" through North America to India.

You will soon participate in a simulation of the spice trade. Most of you will be spice buyers, and a few of you will sell spices, ships, and trading roods.

To the buyers: You each have one hundred ducats. In order to reach the spice sellers, you must have a ship. These ships, which you may buy from the shipbuilder, cost two hundred ducats each. So you must join forces; you must find partners who will help you, since no one by himself has enough money to buy a ship. Once you have a ship, you must have trading goods. Each shipload of trading goods costs fifty ducats, and is good for ten toothpicks once you reach the spice sellers. You may buy these from the ship outfitter.

When you have your ship and your trading goods, you may start. Your teacher will give you the steps to follow.

After the simulation is finished, you may be curious about the spices we use today. How many can you find in your kitchen? On a grocery shelf? Where do they come from? How are they used? Do they have any essential vitamins or minerals? How do they taste, and smell?

100 DUCATS	50 DUCATS
100 DUCATS	50 DUCATS
100 DUCATS	50 DUCATS
100 DUCATS	50 DUCATS
500 DUCATS	500 DUCATS

FIGURE 8-3: Spice Trade Money

ONE SAILING SHIP Cost: 200 ducats	ONE SAILING SHIP Cost: 200 ducats
ONE SAILING SHIP Cost: 200 ducats	ONE SAILING SHIP Cost: 200 ducats

FIGURE 8-4: Ship Cards

ONE SHIPLOAD OF TRADING GOODS Cost: 50 ducats	ONE SHIPLOAD OF TRADING GOODS Cost: 50 ducats
ONE SHIPLOAD OF TRADING GOODS Cost: 50 ducats	ONE SHIPLOAD OF TRADING GOODS Cost: 50 ducats

FIGURE 8-5: Trading Goods Cards

SAFE TRIP	SAFE TRIP
SAFE TRIP	SAFE TRIP
SAFE TRIP	SAFE TRIP
STORM—Lose all your cargo. Ship and crew return home safely.	STORM—Your ship is SUNK. All crew is saved and returned home.
PIRATES—Lose all your cargo. Ship and crew return home safely.	PIRATES take all of your cargo and sink your ship. Crew are returned home safely.

FIGURE 8-6: Travel Hazards Cards

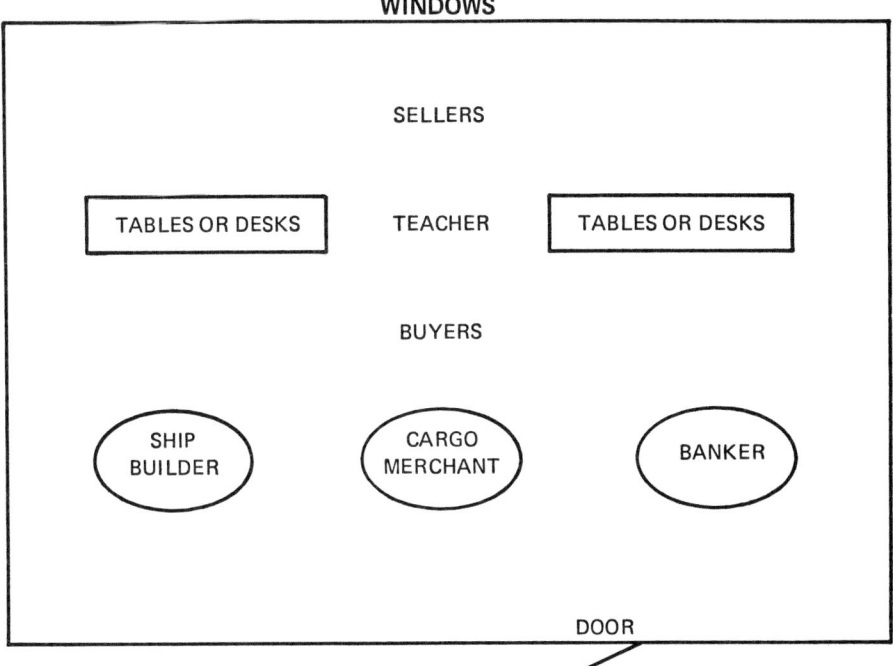

FIGURE 8-7: Typical Classroom Set-up

INFLUENCE

Resume. This is an interaction simulation in which students compete for points. They have a chance to give points to their neighbors or subtract from their neighbors' points.

Grade levels. Fifth, sixth, and seventh grades.

Teaching objectives. (1) To give students a chance to show their friendliness and/or hostility toward their neighbors in the classroom in a non-threatening way. (2) To pinpoint some students with consistently friendly (or positive) attitudes and consistently unfriendly (or negative) attitudes. (3) To indicate differences in attitudes when students choose their own neighbors compared to when they do not. (4) To give the teacher an understanding of social interaction within the classroom.

Materials needed. Thirty-six cardboard or tagboard arrows, approximately twenty centimeters by five centimeters. These arrows are numbered from one to thirty-six, on both sides. One side has a large arrow on it. The other has just the number. (See Figure 8-8.)
(2) Thirty-six cards numbered from one to thirty-six.

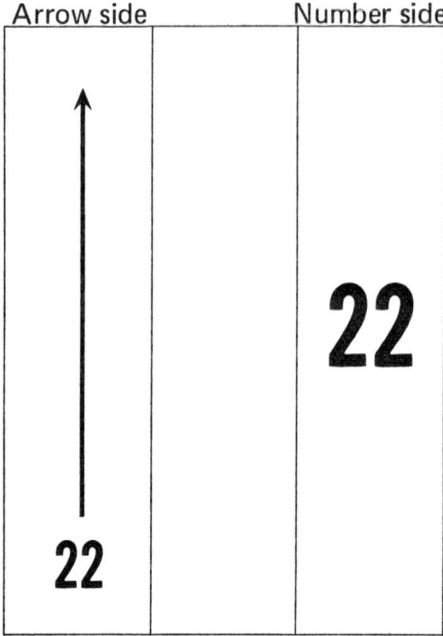

FIGURE 8-8: Examples of the Arrows

Getting ready. (1) Distribute the arrows to the students, at random. Each student should have one arrow. Leftovers are laid aside.

(2) Appoint a student recorder, who does not participate.

(3) Explain the rules. They are as follows:

Students may place their arrows flat on their desks, in five different directions: (1) arrow pointing forward; (2) arrow pointing backward; (3) arrow pointing left; (4) arrow pointing right; (5) number side up (doesn't matter which way it points).

Or the student may hold the arrow vertically in two directions: (1) arrow pointing up; (2) arrow pointing down.

Students are competing for points. They earn points when a numbered card is drawn, as follows: (1) Ten points are given to the student with the same number as the card drawn, if he has his arrow flat on his desk (no matter which way it is pointing). (2) Five points are given for each neighbor (front, back, sides) who has his arrow pointing to the person with the number drawn. (3) If the person with the same number as on the card drawn has his number side up (no arrow showing), he gets five points, and his neighbors nothing. (4) If a person with the same number as the card drawn has his arrow pointing up (vertically), he gets five points and each neighbor gets five points also, regardless of which way their arrow is placed. (5) If the person with the same number as the card drawn has his arrow pointing down, he gets ten points and his neighbors each get five points subtracted from their score, regardless of which way their arrows are placed. (6) As an exception to # 5, if a neighbor to the person with the arrow pointing down has his number side up (no arrow showing), he does not lose or gain points.

To play. (1) Ask the students to sit in numbered consecutive order in rows. (#1 is first in the first row, #2 is second, and so on.)

(2) Give the students fifteen to thirty seconds in which to choose how to place their arrows on their desks. After the time is up, they may not move them.

(3) Draw a card and announce the number. Give points to the student with the number drawn and add or subtract points as needed for the neighbors. Neighbors are students directly in front and behind, and directly to the left or right; diagonal neighbors do not count. Students on ends of rows and on side rows will have fewer neighbors.

(4) Recorder should note on a sheet which students have their arrows pointing up and which have theirs pointing down, regardless of whether they were given points for that round. Students with arrows placed flat on their desks need not be noted.

(5) Go through ten rounds of drawing numbers.

(6) At the end of the tenth round, ask students to move into desks and choose their own neighbors. Give them a three-minute time limit in which to do this. They need not move if they do not wish to.

(7) Go through ten more rounds.

(8) Announce the total points for each student. Student with the most points is the winner.

(9) Strategies will develop as the students learn the game. Some classes will see advantages to having all arrows pointing the same direction, for example.

Debriefing. After the simulation has ended, initiate a class discussion using the following or similar questions:

1. Did you always follow the same pattern in placing your arrow? (That is, always to the left, right, etc.)
2. Did you pay attention to how your neighbors' arrows were pointing?
3. Did you change the direction of your own arrow, after seeing your neighbors'?
4. Who tried to exert influence?

5. When you were allowed to choose your neighbor, did your pattern of placing your arrows change? If so, how?
6. How did you feel when your neighbor placed his arrow pointing down?
7. How did you feel when your neighbor placed his arrow pointing up?
8. Does this game tell you anything about how you influence your neighbor, on the playground or elsewhere?

Teacher conclusions.

It is possible that this simulation will you something about the social interaction of your class. You might want to examine the list compiled by the recorder and ask yourself these questions, or even discuss them with your class:

How many positive (arrow pointing up) moves were made, total?

How many negative (arrow pointing down) moves were made, total?

Were there more positive than negative moves, or vice versa? Could you draw any conclusions about the class interaction?

What student(s) had the most positive moves?

What student(s) had the most negative moves?

What students never made a positive or negative move?

Were there consistencies? Or did a single student use both types of moves?

Were there changes from positive to negative or vice versa as the game changed in the middle?

How did the second half differ from the first half?

A warning: Some students will treat this as a game (and rightly so), and it is possible that some positive or negative moves will be part of the game strategy and not necessarily indicate positive or negative feelings toward others.

Variation.

1. Change the point scale. For instance, give a negative move more points than a positive move, or vice versa.

Assignment.

Consider how influence is made in "real" life: through the use of money, power, position, or personality. Report.

CHAPTER 9

Simplified Ways to Make Your Own Simulations and Games

It's Not So Hard. Here's Why.

Creating and designing your own simulation or game can be a very rewarding experience. It really isn't all that hard, because as you try out your ideas, you can modify, add, subtract, as you go along. You and the class learn as much from a simulation or game that doesn't work well as from one that works perfectly, I have found. If you are still uncertain of your feet in game design, follow some of the steps in this chapter.

Play Some First.

Before doing too much on your own, try some games and simulations first. Try a variety of simulations to get the feel of them—from role-playing and simple simulations and games to the very complicated simulations that cover a spectrum of teaching areas. If you can't do it with your class, it might be possible with your family. Failing that, read through them carefully and imagine how they might go. Also, it is of help to try a number of commercial board games and see the variety offered.

Advantages of Making Your Own Simulations and Games.

There are many advantages to making your own. The foremost is that you can tailor a game or simulation to fit your own class—their abilities, their maturity level, their strong and weak points. The second is related: you can create simulations to fit problem areas that your class encounters. You will see times when your class is bored with a topic or lesson, and you can liven it with a simulation that fits. The third advantage is that as the author you know the rules and procedure. You don't have to stop and look up a rule in the middle of a game. You can create new rules or clarify existing ones as you go.

Re-design Some Existing Games. Do Some Variations.

A good way to begin designing your own simulations or games is to take a commercial simulation and re-design it. Cut out parts, add new ones, or do a variation. This way you can get a feel for designing simulations without running into major headaches such as "How do I work this situation out?" In most of the simulations in this book, I have suggested some variations.

How One of My Simulations (REPORTERS) Was Developed.[1]

Simulations will change and develop of themselves as you try them with successive classes. Note the simulation REPORTERS given in Chaper 6. I first created REPORTERS as a simple research assignment in which students would pretend they were foreign correspondents. Several students in this class were consistently late in turning in papers, so I decided to encourage promptness by setting a rate of payment, depending upon when they turned the news story in.

I made a wall chart upon which I could record the amount of pay given each student. This was as far as I had intended to go—I supposed that seeing their imagined pay recorded on the chart would be reward enough. But one boy, about half-way through, came to me and stated, half-seriously, "I'm going on strike until I get my money."

I thought this over, and that evening I bought a packet of *Monopoly* money from a local toy store. The students were then paid in this paper money, which they took home or gave away, as they wished.

That was as far as I went with that year's class.

The following year, I introduced the same social studies unit, proposing to pay students in play money after they had finished a certain number of news reports. Some of them wanted their pay at once. "All right," I said, "but you will have to be paid in Argentine pesos." I dittoed some pesos and paid them. (Actually, the toy store was sold out of *Monopoly* money, and I used this to stall until I could obtain more.) The Argentine pesos introduced students to the concept of international exchange, since a peso at that time was worth almost half a cent in U.S. money.

---

[1]This section was originally printed in *Instructor*, March, 1970, page 50, entitled "Outcomes from a Social Studies Project."

But this class was not merely satisfied to receive play money. They asked, "What is it good for?"

My student teacher suggested a market place, or an auction, at which the students could spend their money. So an auction date was announced.

Now other complications arose.

Free Enterprise. Since our play money now had value, all sorts of private buying and selling transactions began: pencils, pens, stamps, baseball cards, marbles, and other items were exchanged for play money. One enterprising boy asked for scraps of paper from our art scrap box, made a dozen or so small note pads, and sold them.

Counterfeiting. Since the play money (after I had bought more) was the same as *Monopoly* money from the game, some students began to bring *Monopoly* money from home. I had to call all of the play money back in, and backstamp all of the bills with a large distinctive "R" to prevent such counterfeiting.

Banks. Two students became bankers, renting as their "safe" a portion of my closet which could be locked, and charging customers for the privilege of keeping their money there so it could not be stolen.

Theft Protection. Many students preferred not to use the banking facilities, but some complained to me about the loss of money from their desks. I suggested that a way to keep track of bills would be to record their serial numbers. This meant that serial numbers had to be placed on them, in special ink.

Inflation. Every once in a while we played a "College Bowl" game in science. "Why can't the winners be paid in our play money?" asked the students. The class voted in favor of such action, and set the payment at $500 per winner ($1500 for a team of three). I warned them of the dangers of adding to the supply of money, but they had to learn for themselves. After four games, they saw how inflation (through an increase in the amount of money in circulation) can set in—"Free Enterprise" prices rose drastically.

We had two class auctions. I was the auctioneer. The first was after the fifth cablegram, the day before the start of spring vacation, and the second one was at the close of the unit. I supplied foreign stamps, candy bars, odds and ends from cereal box offers, and a few extra fossils I had. The auctions were exciting and the bidding was fierce and competitive. (A year later, the father of one of my students, a professional auctioneer, conducted the auction.)

As it has evolved by the actions of my classes, my original unit has taken on many new dimensions, expanding from a simple social studies assignment to a unit involving many factors of practical economics and finance.

Steps to Follow in Making Your Own.

Here are some of the steps I follow when I create a simulation or game. The order is more or less as I go through:

1. Define the problem or situation.
2. How could students best experience it?
3. Decide upon the grade or age level.
4. Set the teaching objectives.
5. Get all of the steps clear in mind.
6. Decide upon the pieces and component parts needed.
7. Decide how to set it up.
8. Decide upon the rules of play and how a winner is determined.
9. Clarify the debriefing.
10. Make a working model.
11. Field test the model.
12. Revise it as needed.
13. Field test it again if major revisions were made.

1. *Define the problem.* The problem or situation is where I start. I look for places in the curriculum where students are having trouble understanding the concepts, where they are bored or turned off, or where a simulation or game might introduce a topic or culminate a unit.

2. *How could students best experience it?* Next I decide what type of simulation or game might best dramatize or illuminate the situation. Sometimes role-playing is best. Another time it might be a board game. It all depends upon the situation.

3. *Decide upon the grade or age level.* This step only applies where more than one grade or age or maturity level is involved. When I was teaching fifth and sixth grade social studies to four classes a day, sometimes a game or simulation would work better for one grade level than for another.

4. *Set the teaching objectives.* Most often at the beginning I have only one teaching objective in mind; usually it is one concept. This is an important step. Always ask yourself, "What is it I am trying to teach?" It will clarify the working of your simulation or game.

5. *Get all the steps clearly in mind.* It is essential to work out in your mind or on paper what the students will do first, what second, and so on. Until you can do this, it is useless to go further. This step is the core of any simulation or game.

6. *Decide upon the pieces and components needed.* The components (board, pieces, dittoes, forms) are essential parts of the game or simulation. You may start with a few, and find as you test it out that others (particularly forms and charts) will help it go more smoothly.

7. *Decide how to set the game or simulation up.* How will you introduce the game or simulation to your students? Will background material be necessary, or will you just begin? Will you use a pre-test? These are questions to be answered here. This step is connected to the following one.

8. *Decide upon the rules of play and how a winner (if any) is determined.* I have found that rules of play are items that frequently need revision or clarification as I test the simulation. I start with a minimum of rules, and as students participate, I change them as deemed necessary. Whether or not a simulation has a winner is determined in part by the type. Not all simulations need winners.

9. *Clarify the debriefing.* Decide how you and your students will evaluate the game or simulation. Go back to your teaching objectives and try to form questions that will give you an idea whether or not the objectives were accomplished. Also evaluate the strategies and rules of the game itself. You may want to ask for suggestions about improvement.

10. *Make a working model.* Try it with your class and see how it goes. If you can, it is helpful to let another teacher try it also.

11. *Field test the model.* Try it with your class and see how it goes. If you can, it is helpful to let another teacher try it also.

12. *Revise it as needed.* Make changes as indicated by the flow and direction of the simulation itself, as well as the debriefing evaluation. Student interest and enthusiasm will also help you revise.

13. *Field test the simulation again if major revisions were made.* You may need to test your revised model, though it may be with next year's class, or with the class of the teacher across the hall (if you can talk fast enough). Sometimes I have done the revised simulation with the same class, to get their reactions.

Some Do's in Making Your Own Simulation or Game.

My list of do's is short, because most of them are covered in the foregoing:

1. Motivation is important.
2. Look at the weak points as you test.
3. Ask yourself, "What are the players' objectives?"

1. *Motivation is important.* Sometimes just the playing of the game or simulation itself will generate its own enthusiasm and motivation.

But this is not necessarily the case. You may want to consider ways to motivate the class so that they will really want to play the game. This is especially true if the topic is one unfamiliar to them. I recall one simulation of the Middle Ages I tried (not my own) that did not work well simply because I had not spent time with the class in background and motivation.

2. *Look at the weak points as you field test.* If the simulation does not seem to be going well as you try it, see if you can find out why. It is frequently helpful just to stop and start over. Go back and begin again with new rules or procedures. Or perhaps you may want to take notes for later revisions as you observe the simulation in action. Look for students who are unsure of themselves and what to do and for the ones who are doing nothing; listen to the questions students ask you. If you get the same questions over and over, this is an indication that rule clarification is needed. Sometimes just a change in physical arrangement will help. Sometimes a form or chart will do it. Or maybe you need to ditto the rules or write them on the chalkboard so students will remember them more easily.

3. *Ask yourself, "What are the players' objectives?"* Pretend you are a player. What will you be aiming for? What goals will you have in mind? Will you be interested in accumulating money, or cards, or points? Will you be asking for cooperation of other players? Or will you be seeking to dominate them (power)? Or are you unclear just what your goal is? If the latter is the case, some revisions are necessary in the rules, or the background, or the procedure.

Some Don'ts in Making Your Own Simulation or Game.

Rather than give you someone else's list of don'ts, I'm going to list some of the bad examples from my own experience:

1. Don't start with the pieces and try to make a game to fit.
2. Don't ignore the teaching objectives.
3. Don't make it too complicated.
4. Don't let part of the class watch (at least for long).
5. Don't write incomplete or unclear directions.

1. *Don't start with the pieces and try to make a game to fit.* I had a number of hardboard squares left over from a project, and decided to make a game to use them up. It just didn't work. I really didn't have

any other objective in mind, except to make use of the squares. (I also once tested a commercial simulation that had beautiful pieces, boards, and components, but the objectives and rules were vague. I wondered if this had not also been the case.)

2. *Don't design a neat simulation or game with planned moves, and ignore the teaching objectives—there may not be any.* I set up a nice game entitled *Tramp Spacer* with distances between the stars calculated, and times (moves) from one to the other. But when I tried to write teaching objectives, I couldn't think of any. I had to drop it.

3. *Don't make a simulation so full of papers, pieces, and other components that is is unwieldy.* I designed a farming game set in the late 1800's, with checks, currency, silver dollars, gold coins, and with pieces for cattle, sheep, horses, hay, and with maps. Even with a small group (ten students) there were just too many components. It might yet work with up to four students—but no more.

4. *Don't design a simulation that will work with only a portion of the class.* If a teacher has thirty students, and only ten can play the simulation at once, what will the others do? (The teacher could, I know, do three simulations at once, provided there are aides or student teachers to help, but not many of us can do that.) I designed a simulation for a small group, but eventually enlarged it so all could participate in some form. I recently examined a commercial classroom kit that included two beautifully made simulations. The first was to be played to introduce the topic. It played well, but at the most only twelve student could be involved at once. A teacher would have to order more copies to include the entire class.

5. *Don't write directions that are incomplete or unclear.* It is easy, when writing directions and rules, to take things for granted, and to end up with steps omitted or unclear. When you know how the game goes, you may assume the players know all the steps that you are taking for granted. This is like telling you to go from A to C and assuming that you will go through B without actually making it clear that you *must* go through B to get to C.

Why Not Develop One with Your Class? Do a "Game Game."

One good learning situation is the collective invention of a game in the classroom. The class should be one that has played a number of games and simulations already. The content then is the process of making the game or simulation. The culmination is playing it.

The beginning of the process is a choice of topic. It could grow out of social studies, language, reading, or science lesson, or from a particular interest of the students.

Perhaps a simple game could develop, so that each student could make his own to take home and play with his family.

In doing this process, the class could be divided into separate committees. Or a small group of "game-minded" students would work on it by themselves.

I should emphasize that even though a workable game does not develop, students will have learned a great deal in the process . . . not so much about designing a game as about the content, the "real world," which is used in the game. Also the give and take, the class interaction, the sense of working toward a common goal, will be a gain.

Developing Simulations and Games for the Market.

If you should design a game or simulation that you think would have value for others you might want to develop it further as a commercial venture. Developing a game is much harder than designing it. In the development, several classes should try it out so that any problem areas can be spotted and changed. It is also a good idea to let another teacher try it—thus the gaps in the rules will show up.

The chances of breaking into the board game market with a major company are very slim. Most of the companies that publish games sold in retail stores introduce only one new one a year. Yours will have to be outstanding to make it.

But the commercial market for simulations is still open. The commercial simulation companies are small, and their output per game is small, but they do introduce many new ones each year. Once you have developed a simulation, send a working copy to one of the companies mentioned in the following chapter, or others. You may be rewarded by seeing it published.

I have never worried about a company taking my idea when I send them a copy of a game, but if you are concerned about it, send another copy to yourself by registered mail and keep it sealed in a safe place.

There are, at the time of writing, several areas and levels relatively untouched by simulations. One is the primary grades. There are almost no simulations for grades one through three on the market. Someone who could invent some simple simulations in almost any topic for these grades ought to have a sale. Also some teaching areas such as science, music, language, reading, and art, are relatively untouched at any grade level. On the other hand, social studies is well covered, almost saturated. But at any level, any teaching area, good simulations are still wanted.

CHAPTER 10

How to Quickly Locate Good Simulations and Games

Good Simulations I Have Used.[1]

The games listed below are some I have tried in the classroom, and found effective for fifth and sixth grades:

BOXCARS (Interact).[2] This involves transportation and trading on European railroads. $8.00. Grades 4 to 9.

DESIGN (Interact). This is an excellent simulation on designing and furnishing a home. It keeps student interest and involvement. In my opinion, it is one of the top simulations in economics and career education. $20 a classroom set. Grades 5 to 12.

DISCOVERY (Interact). Students are travelers to the New World, founding colonies and struggling to survive. $12 a classroom set. Grades 5 to 8.

ENERGY X (EMI). This is one of the few science simulations on the market in the area of energy conservation. $19.50. Grades 5 through high school.

GOMSTON (EMI). This is a science simulation involving pollution. $25.00. Grades 5 to high school. This works well in today's classes.

HUMANUS (Simile II). This is a future studies simulation, best for junior high and up, though mature 6th grades could use it.

IMPORT (Simile II, also EMI). This is a simple trading simulation. $10.00. Grades 4 and 5.

---

[1] Eight other simulations (my own) are listed in Appendix 2.

---

[2] See the section on manufacturers and distributors in this chapter for addresses and abbreviations.

MAHOPA (Interact). This is a simulation about Indian tribes. $12.00. Grades 5 to 8.

NATIONALISM (EduGame). Students are leaders of seven fictitious nations. Diplomacy is used. $1.50. For mature 6th grades through 12th.

NEW CITY TELEPHONE COMPANY (Simile II, also EMI). Students are managers of a telephone company in a large city. They must make many decisions. $15.00. Grades 5 and 6.

PHOENIX (EMI). Students are survivors of a world-wide catastrophe. They receive instructions from a cassette tape. $12.00. Grades 5 and 6.

PIONEERS (Interact). Wagon trains try to reach Oregon safely. Many decisions, also mapwork. $20 a classroom set. Grades 5 to 8.

POWDERHORN (Simile II, also EMI). Students find out about the uses and abuses of power as they trade goods in a pioneer society. (A similar game, STAR POWER, is a classic. It is for upper grades and adults.) $12.50. Grades 5 and 6.

WAR TIME (EduGame). Students are members of four fictitious nations, which may go to war. $1.50. Grades: mature 6th to 12th.

WORLD (Interact). This simulation introduces middle-grade students to world politics. Works well. $20 per classroom set. Grades 6 through 9.

Good Board Games and Card Games I Have Used.

The following board and card games are good for small groups of students. A few have classroom versions for larger groups. These games are good for extra interest, for free time, for motivation. Have you ever tried a game day with your class, in which they play these types of games?

Most of these games may be purchased at toy and hobby stores. Prices may vary.

AIRPORT (EMI). A board game concerned with the operation of airlines. Two to six players. $9.00. Grades 5 to adult.

AMERICAN CIVIL WAR (SPI). A board game using armies and navies of the Civil War. Two to four players. $8.00. Grades 6 to adult.

AMERICAN REVOLUTION (SPI). A board game using armies and navies of the colonists, Britain, and France. Two to four players. $8.00. Grades 6 to adult.

BEAT INFLATION (Avalon Hill). $10.00. Grades 5 and up.

BUSINESS STRATEGY (Avalon Hill, also EMI). A good game in the area of economics. Two to four players. $10.00 Mature 6th grades to adult.

CAREERS (EMI). Players choose occupations, participate in the working world. Two to six players. $7.25. Grades 5 to adult.

DECIMETER (Lawhead). A board game using the metric system. Two to six players. $11.00. Grades 4 and up. (Two levels of difficulty.)

DIPLOMACY (Avalon Hill). A board game of international negotiations. Four to seven players. $12.00. Grades 6 to adult.

MASTERPIECE (Parker Brothers, also EMI). A board game that teaches about works of art. Two to eight players. $8.00. Grades 5 to adult.

MONOPOLY (Parker Brothers). A classic that all students should know. Two to eight players. About $8.00. Grades 4 to adult.

ORIGINS OF WORLD WAR II (Avalon Hill, also EMI). A game of diplomacy, pre-World War II. Two to six players; also classroom. $10.00. Grades 5 to adult.

PIRATE CACHE (Lawhead). A mathematics board game that teaches coordinates, positive and negative numbers. Two to six players. $11.00. Grades 5 and up.

PREDATOR (Ampersand Press, 2603 Grove Street, Oakland, CA 94612). A card game of food chains in a forest. Two to six players. Grades 5 to adult.

1776 (Avalon Hill, also EMI). A board game of the American Revolution. Two to eight players. $10.00. Grades 6 to adult.

THE STOCK MARKET GAME (Avalon Hill, also EMI). A good game involving the ups and downs of the stock market. Two to six players. Also a version for entire classroom. $10.00. Mature 5th grades to adult.

THIRD REICH (Avalon Hill, EMI). A board game of World War II in Europe. Two to six players. $11.00. Mature 6th grades to adult.

ULCERS (EMI). A board game involved in the hiring of personnel. Two to six players. $10.00. Mature 5th grades to adult.

THE WINNING TOUCH (EMI). Teaches multiplication facts. A board game that is widely used. One to four players. $7.00. Grades 3 and up.

Good Sources of New Simulations and Games: Game Publishers and Dealers.

The publishers and distributors listed below are sources of the games and simulations previously listed. They are also constantly publishing new games and simulations, and by the time this book is published will have many new ones that are not mentioned here. You might want to write for their catalogs and price lists.

AVALON HILL, 4517 Harford Road, Baltimore MD 21214. Simulations and board games sold mostly in retail stores, though you can buy direct from them.

EDUCATIONAL MANPOWER INC. (EMI), P.O. Box 4272-D, Madison, WI 53711. This is a major distributor of many different games and simulations. They have two catalogs: one for elementary grades, and one for upper grades and high school.

EDU-GAME, P.O. Box 1144, Sun Valley, CA 91352. They sell simulations and puzzles for $1.50. Most of their simulations are for junior high level, but some mature sixth grades can use them. Their puzzles are good at 5th and 6th grade level.

GAMES CENTRAL, Wheeler Street, Cambridge, MA 02138. One of the first to publish simulations. They have them in the $15 to $60 price range.

INTERACT, P.O. Box 262, Lakeside, CA 92040. They publish a wide variety of simulations in a price range from $10 to $20.

LAWHEAD PRESS, 900 E. State Street, Athens, OH 45701. They publish board games for schools in a medium price range ($11.00).

PARKER BROTHERS, Salem, MA. An old commercial publisher of games for retail stores.

SIMILE II, P.O. Box 910, Del Mar, CA 92014. They publish social studies simulations in a medium price range.

SIMULATIONS PUBLICATIONS INC. (SPI) 44 East 23rd Street, New York, NY 10010. They publish mostly war board games, and also two magazines of military history and gaming.

STEM, P.O. Box 393, Provo, UT 84601. They sell simulations for $2.00 and $3.00 in a variety of titles.

S-T-E-P AHEAD, INC., 1231 Olive Street, Eugene, OR 97401. They publish board games in reading readiness for kindergarten through fourth grade.

Appendixes

PRACTICAL STATISTICAL DATA ON SIMULATIONS

I. Statistics on individual simulations and games.[1]

Game	Pre-test Post-test (class mean)		Gain	No. students who showed gain.	"Did it help you understand this career?" % Yes.
COUNCIL	65%	71%	6%	58%	87%
DESIGN	33%	49%	16%	73%	84%
MERCHANT	55%	68%	13%	79%	(not asked)
POLICE PATROL	(pre and post tests not given)				89%
Real Estate	"	"	"		71%
Construction Jobs	"	"	"		65%
Salespersons	"	"	"		90%
Wheatacres	"	"	"		89%

[1]Simulations and games listed in CAPITAL LETTERS are available commercially. Those that are underlined are in this book.

II. Survey on entire project.

Question: "How much did you learn from this project?"

	Very little		Some	A lot	
	1	2	3	4	5
Class I (17 students)	6%	0	6%	12%	76%
Class II (19 students)	0	0	31%	16%	53%
Class III (23 students)	0	4%	13%	57%	26%
Class IV (24 students)	0	4%	4%	25%	67%
All classes (83 students)	1%	2%	13%	30%	54%

Question: How much did you enjoy this project?"

	Very little		Some	A lot	
	1	2	3	4	5
Class I (17 students)	12%	0	17%	12%	59%
Class II (19 students)	0	16%	11%	5%	68%
Class III (23 students)	4%	4%	13%	35%	44%
Class IV (24 students)	4%	9%	13%	17%	57%
All classes (83 students)	5%	7%	14%	18%	56%

III. Survey of control classes and experimental classes.

Question: How interesting are your classes?

	Very int.	Kind of inter.	So-so	Not int.	I hate it.
Career Education (Experimental)	47%	33%	18%	2%	0
Career Education (Control)	24%	15%	38%	17%	6%
All 12 subjects (Experimental)	49.8%	23.2%	15.2%	4.7%	7.1%
All 12 subjects (Control)	22.75%	25.25%	33.4%	8.7%	9.9%

APPENDIX 2

OTHER SIMULATIONS DEVELOPED BY THE AUTHOR

CONTRACTORS (Interact, P.O. Box 262, Lakeside, CA 92040). Students are managers of contracting firms making bids for construction projects. $20 a set. Grades 5 to 8.

COUNCIL (Interact). This simulates meetings of a city council. Useful in studying about local governments. $20 a classroom set. Grades 5 to 8.

EXPLORERS 1 (Simile II, P.O. Box 910, Del Mar, CA 92014). Students are exploring for new lands. It also includes early colonial period. $4.50. Grades 4 to 8.
EXPLORERS 2 (Simile II). Students are South American explorers. $4.50. Grades 5 to 8.

FLIGHT (Interact). Students are airplane pilots racing over a map. Teaches map symbols, scale, etc. $8 a set. Grades 4 to 8.

HOMESTEAD (Interact). Students are farmers in the old West in the late 1800's. $20 a classroom set. Grades 5 to 8.

MERCHANT (Interact). Students are owners and operators of general stores in the early 1900's. $20 a classroom set. Grades 5 to 8.

ROARING CAMP (Simile II). Students are gold miners trying to strike it rich. $10.00. Grades 4 to 8.

APPENDIX 3

SIMULATIONS AND GAMES, BY GRADE LEVEL.

X = recommended grades. y = will work. - = not recommended.

Title	Page	3	4	5	6	7	8	9	High School	College & Adult
AMBASSADORS	152	-	-	y	X	X	X	X	-	-
ANDESIA	31	-	-	X	X	X	X	X	y	y
BAL. OF POWER	67	-	-	-	X	X	X	y	-	-
BLUE WOD. CO.	74	-	-	-	X	X	X	X	X	y
CEN. AM. SUMMIT	38	-	-	y	X	X	X	X	X	y
CL. STOCK MARKET	103	-	-	y	X	X	X	X	y	y
COMPUTER SUB.	180	y	X	X	X	y	-	-	-	-
CONST. JOBS	111	y	X	X	y	-	-	-	-	-
DOME CITY	149	-	-	-	X	X	X	X	X	X
GALACTICA	97	-	-	y	X	X	X	y	y	-
HOW MANY?	170	-	X	X	X	X	y	-	-	-
INDIAN TREATY	41	-	-	y	X	X	X	X	y	y
INFLUENCE	197	-	y	X	X	X	y	-	-	-
LANDOSA	87	-	-	X	X	X	X	X	y	y
MAKE A METER	179	y	X	X	X	y	y	y	-	-
PANATINA	57	-	-	y	X	X	X	X	y	y
REAL ESTATE	116	y	X	X	X	y	-	-	-	-
REPORTERS	161	-	y	X	X	X	-	-	-	-
SALESPERSONS	123	-	-	X	X	X	X	y	-	-
SPICE TRADE	190	y	X	X	X	X	y	-	-	-
STAMP DETECTIVES	165	-	y	X	X	y	-	-	-	-
STRAWBERRY FARM	29	X	X	X	X	-	-	-	-	-
VOYAGEURS	185	y	X	X	X	y	y	-	-	-
WHEATACRES	132	-	-	X	X	X	X	X	X	X
YARD/M. FR. GAME	171	-	X	X	X	y	-	-	-	-

APPENDIX 4

SIMULATIONS AND GAMES, BY SUBJECT AREA

X=major areas; y=minor areas.

Title	Page	Anthropol.	Career Ed.	Economics	Geogr.	History	Lang., Rdg.	Math.	Pol. Sci.	Soc. Interaction
AMBASSADORS	152		y		y	X			X	
ANDESIA	31						y		X	y
BAL. OF POWER	67								X	y
BLUE WOD. CO.	74		X	X				y		y
CEN. AM. SUMMIT	38			X	X		y		X	y
CL. STOCK MARKET	103			X				y		y
COMPUTER SUB.	180							X		
CONST. JOBS	111		X	X						
DOME CITY	149		X				y			y
GALACTICA	97			X			y			X
HOW MANY?	170							X		
INDIAN TREATY	41	X				X	y			y
INFLUENCE	197									X
LANDOSA	87		y	X				y	X	
MAKE A METER	179							X		
PANATINA	57			y	X				X	
REAL ESTATE	116		X	y			y			
REPORTERS	161		y		X	X	X			
SALESPERSONS	123		X	X			y			X
SPICE TRADE	190			X	X	X				y
STAMP DETECTIVES	165					y	X			
STRAWBERRY FARM	29		y							y
VOYAGEURS	185				X	X	y			
WHEATACRES	132		X	X		y		X		
YARD/M. FR. GAME	171							X		

BIBLIOGRAPHY

Abt, Clark C. *Serious Games.* New York: The Viking Press. 1970.

Bower, Eli M., Benjamin, Kersa, Fine, Amy, and Carlson, Joy. *Learning to Play: Playing to Learn.* Berkeley: U. of Calif. School of Ed. 1974.

Brady, Maxine. *The Monopoly Book.* New York: David McKay. 1974

Chapman, Katherine, and Cousins, Jack E. *Simulation/Games in Social Studies: A Report.* Boulder, Colo.: ERIC/CHESS. 1974.

Chapman, Katherine, Davis, James E., and Meier, Andrea. *Simulation/Games in Social Studies: What Do We Know?* Boulder, Colo.: ERIC/CHESS. 1974.

Charles, Cheryl, and Stadsklev, Ron, eds. *Learning with Games.* Boulder, Colo.: Social Science Education Consortium. 1973.

Chartier, Myron. *How to Teach with Simulation Games.* Pasadena, Calif.: Associates in Human Communication. 1974.

Duke, Richard D. *Gaming: The Future's Language.* New York: John Wiley & Sons. 1974.

Gibbs, G.I., ed. *Handbook of Games and Simulation Exercises.* Beverly Hills, Calif.: Sage Publications, Inc. 1974.

Glazier, Ray. *How to Design Educational Games.* Cambridge, Mass.: Abt Associates, Inc. 1969.

Gordon, Alice Kaplan. *Games for Growth.* Palo Alto, Calif.: Science Research Associates. (Undated)

Heyman, Mark. *Simulation Games for the Classroom.* Bloomington, Indiana: Phi Delta Kappa Ed. Foundation. 1975.

Kourilsky, Marilyn. *Beyond Simulation.* Los Angeles, Calif.: Educational Resource Associates. 1974.

Lauffer, Armand. *The Aim of the Game.* New York: Gamed Simulations, Inc. 1973.

Livingston, Samuel A., and Stoll, Clarice. *Simulation Games*. New York: Free Press. 1973.

Maidment, Robert, and Bronstein, Russel H. *Simulation Games, Design and Implementation*. Columbus, Ohio: Charles E. Merrill. 1973.

Pate, Glenn S., and Parker, Hugh A. Jr. *Designing Classroom Simulations*. Belmont, Calif.: Fearon Pub. 1973.

Stadsklev, Ron. *Handbook of Simulation Gaming in Social Education. Part 1: Textbook*. University, Ala.: The University of Alabama. 1974.

Stadsklev, Ron. *Handbook of Simulation Gaming in Social Education. Part 2: Directory*. University, Ala.: The University of Alabama. 1975.

Zuckerman, David W., and Horn, Robert E. *The Guide to Simulations/Games for Education and Training*. Lexington, Mass.: Information Resources, Inc. 1973.

Periodicals:

Simulation/Gaming. Moscow, Idaho. Six issues yearly. Newspaper format.

Simulation & Games. Sage Publications, 275 So. Beverly Drive, Beverly Hills, Calif. 90212. Four issues yearly. Magazine format.

Index